Power Thinking

Power Thinking
Caterina Rando

First published in the United Kingdom and Ireland in 2002 by
Duncan Baird Publishers Ltd
Sixth Floor
Castle House
75–76 Wells Street
London W1T 3QH

Conceived, created and designed by Duncan Baird Publishers

Managing Editor: Judy Barratt
Editors: Peter Bently, Ingrid Court-Jones
Managing Designer: Manisha Patel
Designer: Suzanne Tuhrim
Commissioned Artwork: Emma Harding

British Library Cataloguing-in-Publication Data:
A CIP record for this book is available from the British Library.

ISBN: 1-903296-71-4

10 9 8 7 6 5 4 3 2 1

Typeset in Palatino and TradeGothic
Colour reproduction by Scanhouse, Malaysia
Printed and bound by Imago, Singapore

This book is dedicated to everyone who has ever awoken and wondered if it is really possible to have a life of happiness, fulfilment and purpose, and then got out of bed to create that life.

contents

Introduction 8

CHAPTER ONE: THINK POWER POSITIVE 12

Walk with different steps 14

Exercise 1: Surprise yourself and others 15

How do you think? 16

Whose life is it? 20

Look back to move forward 22

Exercise 2: Identify your imprinting 23

Exercise 3: Look to your future 25

Decide what to change 26

Exercise 4: Six steps to change 27

Centres of power 28

Exercise 5: Build your centres of power 31

Feel different, feel better 32

A space to grow 34

Exercise 6: Create your think tank 35

From thinking to action 36

Exercise 7: Release burdening thoughts 37

CHAPTER TWO: CHOOSE WHERE TO BEGIN 38

Change starts with intention 40

How do you act? 42

Exercise 8: Proactive quiz 43

Eliminate catastrophic thinking 46

Nurture the soil of self 48

Exercise 9: Clear the field 49

CHAPTER THREE: POWER THINKING FITNESS 50

Self-coaching 52

Increase self-awareness 56

Exercise 10: The ultimate questionnaire 57

Develop intuition 60

Exercise 11: Use your sixth sense 61

Challenge glamour and illusion 62

Pick your priorities 64

Frame your ambition 66

Exercise 12: Create an action plan 69

The path of self-devotion 70

Exercise 13: Balance risk and reward 73

Dissolve the inner barriers 74

Exercise 14: A program for change 75

The power of a physical image 78

Exercise 15: Create an image of your desire 79

Where are you now? 82

Exercise 16: The personal review quiz 83

CHAPTER FOUR: THINKING INTO ACTION 84

Making thoughts real 86

Exercise 17: Make your power statements 87

Thoughts into words 88

A time to act 90

Feed on mind and memory 94

Exercise 18: Build a haven of happiness 95

Power decision-making 96

Exercise 19: This or that? 97

The power of gratitude 100

Exercise 20: Practise gratitude 101

Hold a generous heart 104

Choose to approve 106

The helping hand of chance 108

Power from other people 112

Exercise 21: Relationship review 113

A pool of power 116

Exercise 22: Form a power group 117

Here sleeps the champion 118

Exercise 23: Cue your sleeping partner 121

Wings for the angel within 122

Exercise 24: Take your thoughts for a walk 123

CHAPTER FIVE: THE OPEN ROAD 124

The universal timetable 126

Changing gear and turning corners 128

Resilience 130

Exercise 25: Prepare your VIP visit 133

The feel-good imperative 134

Manage your emotions 136

The paradox of struggle 140

Exercise 26: Go pearl-diving 141

Be an explorer 142

Powering ahead 146

Find fulfilment 148

Celebrate! 152

Bibliography 154

Index 155

Acknowledgments 160

introduction

Some years ago I owned and operated a vibrant Italian café in my neighbourhood—the same café my sister Angela opened years before and again operates today. I enjoyed the bustle of the patrons, getting to know everyone who lived nearby, and being part of a small community within a large, urban environment. After a time, though, I began to get restless. I knew I wanted to help people—to make a contribution to their lives. Providing a whole community with a sunny corner in which to enjoy a great cappuccino and fresh salami sandwiches is a true gift—and yet I came to realize that this was not the right work for me.

One day, while I was feeling this way, I was stopped on the street by a woman whom I had first met six months earlier when a mutual friend had suggested that she come to talk to me. At the second, chance meeting, I barely recognized this woman. The first time, she had been unassuming and insecure. Now, she was walking taller, and beaming with confidence and vitality. To my surprise, she thanked me. She explained that, at our previous meeting, I had told her to believe in her capabilities, to figure out what she needed to do to achieve her ambitions, and to go ahead and achieve them! Most of all, she told me, she was thanking me

because I had told her to know that she could be successful and that she could create the life she wanted for herself. I barely recalled the initial conversation; I will never forget the second one. In those brief moments of a chance encounter, her gratitude penetrated my heart, and warmed me with a feeling of contribution that I had never felt before. I never saw her again; I do not remember her name—and yet she sent my life in a whole new direction. My right direction.

When we are open to what the world has to say, we will be sent the messages that will inspire us into action. Your catalyst may come in the form of a chance encounter like mine did—or it may be a movie, a sailboat ride, or a passage of prose. Today, allow this book to serve as your catalyst. I hope that these pages will show you how you can make real the magnificent life that at the moment lives only in your imagination.

The word enthusiasm comes from the Greek word *enthusio,* meaning "the God within you". There is tremendous power within you. To tap into your personal power, bring your enthusiasm to every page in this book. Let your enthusiasm and the book's messages combine to show you how to create a richer, vibrant, more fulfilling life.

Be open to these messages. Many of them are revealed clearly; others may be lying in wait—between the lines, as it were. Your power is unleashed when you let yourself assimilate, reflect upon and implement all the ideas bound within these pages.

Use the book in the way you know will serve you best. You do not have to do the exercises in order; you do not have to do them all; and, if your time is precious, you could do only those that will take a few minutes. The point is that somehow, in some way, you take the first positive step to bring power thinking into your life. Draw strength from the anecdotes I have presented—they are about real people whose lives have changed through the techniques in this book. Let their true stories inspire you.

Although I might reasonably describe myself as an idealist, I am not delusional! I know that many books we buy are set aside barely opened, let alone finished. This book has been created in a way that will make it hard for you to put it down. To entice you to read every page, each subject is covered concisely, and the colourful pages are designed to cultivate rapport—visually and emotionally. Make this book your companion; let it support you, advise you, inspire you to ask insightful questions about how you live your life—and show you how to find the answers.

Finally, the joy and blessing of writing this book are miniscule compared with the huge joy I hope to experience when you tell me how it has impacted your life. Contact me (my details are at the end of the book) and tell me your story, your experiences and your revelations. Let your journey start now.

And finally, from my heart to your heart I send you *potere infinito*—infinite power!

Caterina Rando

think power positive

CHAPTER ONE

Nothing reflects your quality of life more than your thinking. Every waking moment the thoughts keep on coming, no matter what else you are doing. Thinking—the way your mind responds to the world—shapes your beliefs and makes you decide how to act, or not to act. What you think can also feed your fears and fill you with reasons for not making the changes you desire.

The first thing it is important for you to do is break any bad habits of thinking you might have at the moment of picking up this book. It is time to think differently, to think about what is possible, to expand your mind, and then to transform your life.

We begin by looking at how you think now, and building on it. This is the key to determining what course to follow in the future. The more awareness you have about your thinking, the easier it will be for you to turn around that thinking so that it will serve you and your desires for life. You can't reach the stars if you are holding on to the railing. After completing the exercises in this chapter, you will find the stars closer to your grasp.

walk with different steps

Creating who you want to be is like painting a mural—it is never truly finished, and can be endlessly reworked. As the painters of our own lives, most of us do not spend enough time trying new themes, colours and textures. We carry on with the same subjects, the same brushes, the same strokes, the same palette. Over time our self-perception narrows.

A narrow self-perception limits our thinking, our actions, and our life. It makes us think that some things are so definitely beyond our reach that we shouldn't even try to grab them.

One changes from day to day ... every few years one becomes a new being.

GEORGE SAND, FRENCH WRITER

We expect to do well in certain situations but miserably in others. Have you ever refused to sing, even among friends, because you thought you would make a fool of yourself as the notes came out all wrong? Declined a chance to go horse riding, because you didn't see yourself staying on the saddle for more than a few minutes? Balked from giving a speech on some special occasion, because you felt a hurricane of butterflies in your stomach at the very thought of it?

A powerful thing you can do for yourself is to expand your self-perception. Start to do things you previously rejected because they were just "not you". Begin perhaps with something simple yet significant, something you can do on your own without special equipment—like writing a poem or a story. Then learn a skill of some kind, like changing a tire, or typing with all your fingers. Doing new things transforms your sense of who you are and increases your self-respect. Believe me, you are capable of much more than you think you are.

surprise yourself and others

EXERCISE ONE

To begin the process of expanding your self-perception, follow this exercise:

Part A **1. Make a list of qualities or skills** *that you perceive you lack, for example: wit, cooking skills, imagination, bravery, patience, insight. Make the list as long as you like.*

2. Identify one quality *from your list that you would most like to start cultivating.*

3. Think of other people *who have that quality. Meet with them, read about them, and watch them on video. Think how you would be if you had that quality in your own life.*

Part B **1. Make a second list** *of all the things you think you cannot do but would like to—from parachuting or riding to cooking a gourmet meal for friends or winning at chess.*

2. Pick something on this list *that requires the quality chosen in Part A. So if you want to cultivate being braver, pick an activity with an element of bravery.*

3. Now go for it! *If you think you aren't a good cook, throw a banquet. If you think you can't sing, go and see an experienced teacher with a view to taking lessons—he or she will soon be able to gauge your potential. If you think you are a poor swimmer, try an improver class. If you think you can't write, enter a poetry competition.*

Part C **Repeat the process** *until several items are crossed off both lists. Revel in the challenges, however they work out. Enjoy seeing yourself differently—and never look back.*

how do you think?

Aside from your IQ there is another aspect to your thinking that influences every thought you have. I call it your Personal Perspective. This is your basic attitude to life, the way you tend to look at the world, unconsciously and consistently. With its roots in your culture, upbringing and life experiences, your Personal Perspective influences your thoughts, opinions, choices, actions, and ability to make changes.

> *Our life is what our thoughts make it.*
>
> MARCUS AURELIUS, ROMAN EMPEROR, PHILOSOPHER

Reflect on the following different Personal Perspectives. Which one sounds the most like you? While you may sway from one to the other at different times, you have one primary Personal Perspective. This will have its strengths (unless you are a Dissenter), as well as areas of difficulty. Awareness of your Personal Perspective also offers you an opportunity to explore other perspectives to extend your personal horizons.

THE IDEALIST Idealists have faith that things can happen just by believing they can happen. They see the world as a good place, and they are convinced that they can make a contribution to the planet and the lives they touch. **Difficulties:** Idealists tend to believe what they are told and may easily be taken advantage of. They can act before asking questions and gathering all the facts or considering the consequences. They are big dreamers, sometimes too big—meaning that they hope that things will happen rather than having to make them happen. They often stay in unappealing situations for too long because they believe that "things will work out". **Challenge:** Ask more questions, examine your

feelings and pause more often to consider possible outcomes of your actions and beliefs. Think about opportunities before seizing them.

THE REALIST Realists do not sugar-coat anything. They are persuaded by facts and evidence rather than by hypothetical visions or emotional pleas. **Difficulties:** Realists prefer to be sure of success before they take action. They do not act on faith or work things out as they go along. This can limit their openness to opportunities. **Challenge:** Be willing to act without trying to predict down to the last detail how things will work out. Allow yourself to be surprised.

THE PRAGMATIST Pragmatists are often well-balanced people who are flexible in their perspective—they are sometimes realists, sometimes dissenters, sometimes idealists and sometimes questioners. They often acquire a reputation for being reasonable, and for being good judges. However, their outlook is rarely predictable in advance. **Difficulties:** They are unlikely to act on instinct and can go back and forth endlessly before making a decision. This can place relationships under strain. **Challenge:** Limit your thinking time before taking action. Be willing to choose one perspective at a time and go with it. You could also benefit from building up your intuition.

THE QUESTIONER The doubter in the crowd. Questioners have to see something to believe it and will not take your word for it. They often stand on the perimeter and keep their thoughts to themselves. **Difficulties:** Questioners often do not try things because they have not been proven, delaying action until it may be too late. They often let life pass them by. **Challenge:** Allow for the possibility that people and situations sometimes really are as they appear. Don't let your scepticism stop you from taking action whenever it might serve you.

THE STOIC Stoical people show fortitude, but they neither perceive nor express much emotion. Their feelings are difficult to read. They are generally "strong, silent types". **Difficulties:** People find it hard to know them or get close to them. **Challenge:** Seek to be more aware of your feelings, and develop ways to express them. Note the positive effects of reaching out to others emotionally.

THE VISIONARY Visionaries have a unique way of looking

at life. The "energy" of a situation or action—whether it "feels right"—is their most important consideration. **Difficulties:** Their focus on energy means that visionaries can miss or ignore facts, signs and consequences that others see. They can appear to be out of touch with reality. **Challenge:** Focus more on what is practical and realistic—the probable as opposed to the possible. Consider consequences. Take advice from friends who can offer a realistic perspective on important situations.

THE DISSENTER Dissenters do not expect people to be sincere and honest. They do not expect good things to happen to them. **Difficulties:** A dissenter will usually be labelled as negative. Dissenters miss out on many of life's keenest pleasures. **Challenge:** Wake up to the idea that life is wonderful! People can be good and good things can come your way. Release your negativity. Embrace power thinking.

You're not a realist unless you believe in miracles.

ANWAR SADAT, FORMER EGYPTIAN PRESIDENT

check out your Personal Perspective

If you're still unsure of your Personal Perspective, imagine yourself in the following situation. One night you have a really vivid dream that you win the next lottery. The winning numbers are amazingly clear and you remember them when you wake up. Do you: (a) Dismiss it as "just a dream" and forget about it; (b) Think the dream is probably nonsense—but you'll still be curious to see if any of the numbers come up; (c) Doubt whether anything will come of it but see no harm in playing the numbers in the lottery; (d) Get really excited by the dream and buy a lottery ticket on the way to work? Depending on your answer, you are probably: a dissenter (answer a); a questioner (b); a pragmatist (c); or a visionary (d).

whose life is it?

Any unhappiness or the occasional feeling of being "stuck" in our lives often come from an underlying belief that it is somehow not good or right to want what we want, and especially to want more than we have. We think that we should not have strong desires. Pay attention when you hear yourself say "should". This word implies judgment. When you tell yourself you should buy new clothes, clean your kitchen, go to that party, or ask someone over for dinner, it is as if you are responding to what you think is expected of you by society, your parents, your partner, or some other entity, real or imagined.

Life is not about finding yourself, it is about creating yourself.

EDGAR ALLAN POE, AMERICAN WRITER

This belief that we should do certain things and not others is shaped by our birth, upbringing and environment. Other people have moulded our sense of what is right and what is wrong. It is from our parents that we learn that we shouldn't walk on the carpet in our muddy shoes. It is from observing the customs of society in general that we learn to tip in a restaurant, to say "hello" when introduced.

An important early step on the road to power thinking is your decision that you will live your life according to your own standards, not those of other people—although the two will probably coincide to some extent. If you buy something from a store, you are free to try it out and return it if it does not work for you or your home. Similarly, you have the right to test the standards you have acquired from other people, including your parents, since childhood.

The next time you think "I really should do this" or "Oh, I can't do that ... ", pause and ask yourself "Why should I?" or "Why not?" Sometimes the answer will be clear, but at other times less so. It is obvious why you do not walk on a carpet with muddy shoes, because this means someone—and there is a good chance it will be you—has to spend time, energy and maybe money to clean or even replace the carpet. But what is the reason that you shouldn't talk to your boss as an equal? Why shouldn't you remind him of the good work you have done recently in your job? Why shouldn't you ask him for a raise? It is very unlikely that your answer to these questions will be "Because he will get angry and shout at me and maybe threaten to fire me." Even if this did happen, remember that you have the right to ask another question: "Why should I work for someone like that?"

If you want something that feels right for you and does not harm or upset anyone else, then go for it. Believe that you are the author of your own future. If there are things in your life that you are not totally happy about, you are free to look for ways to change them. It is OK to want what you want. Now choose to go get it.

look back to move forward

My grandfathers emigrated to America from southern Italy. Upon arrival one of them sang opera in bistros and the other worked in a lemon processing plant. In addition to a pride in my heritage, a love of Italian culture and cuisine, they also gave me, through my parents, their Italian old world values—a strong sense of family loyalty, the importance of contributing to your community and a belief that to get ahead you have to work very hard for a very long time.

I am never afraid of what I know.

ANNA SEWELL, ENGLISH WRITER

These ideas, passed down to me by words, by example and by psychic energy, I call ancestral imprinting. Imprinting is when outside influences have printed their ideas onto your mind like a spilled glass of red wine on a white tablecloth. You can wash it over and over and it will fade, although a trace of the wine will always remain, for ever part of the cloth. Consider your ancestral imprinting. Does your family descend from factory-workers or farmers, slaves or soldiers, bankers or bakers? Ask yourself which aspects of your character and beliefs might be inherited from your forebears. This exercise is a useful kind of self-analysis that gets you starting to think about who you are, where you come from and what makes you different.

Aside from ancestral imprinting there are other kinds. Parental imprinting often reinforces ancestral imprinting; but, of course, most of us know more about our parents' lives than we could ever discover about our grandparents'. If you saw your parents fighting all the time, you might absorb the idea that marriage and relationships are hurtful.

identify your imprinting

EXERCISE TWO

Begin to explore the imprinting that has impacted on you mentally, spiritually and emotionally by spending some time answering the following questions. You might even choose to discuss these questions with a group of people and see where their imprinting is distinctly the same as or different from yours.

1. *What are the main ideals that distinguish your gender from the other?*
2. *What generation do you belong to? What are the ideals of this generation?*
3. *What generation did your parents belong to? What were the ideals of that generation?*
4. *How might the ideals of your generation and your parents' generation be influenced by historical events such as World War II, the sexual revolution, the women's movement?*
5. *What culture/ethnicity are you and your parents? What are the ideals of that culture?*
6. *What other cultures have you learned about? How have they influenced you?*
7. *What are the ideals of the city or region you live in now? How do you think these ideals have influenced your thinking about how to live your life?*
8. *Do you want to release any ideals or attitudes that you think no longer serve you?*

If your father was over-anxious, or your mother domineering, these things too enter your mindscape as you live.

Gender imprinting—the messages you have received about relations between the sexes—is also very influential. Other factors at work on us include our schooling (maybe even individual teachers), our friends, our work, our accidental encounters with people, ideas and places. Such things colour our perspective, how we see the world, where we are coming from.

Think wrongly, if you please, but in all cases think for yourself.

DORIS LESSING, ENGLISH NOVELIST

This phrase, "where we are coming from", is an important one. It means precisely what it says: where you have come from, your past up to now. You are not your imprinting. After uncovering the prevalent perspectives that have imprinted themselves on you, for your highest good you can either embrace them or reject them.

For example, while sensing something of the Puritan in your perspective, you might resolve to shun austerity and take a more liberal view of duty, marriage and pleasure. It is not exactly that the Puritan is inhabiting you, like a lodger you cannot evict. Puritanism is merely a set of attitudes to which you have immediate access. These might frame themselves automatically in response to certain situations. But they are not the attitudes you must live by. If you feel reluctant to obey some imprinted rallying call inside your head, surely that's a good reason to act differently. If you know where that voice is coming from, you are less likely to make the mistake of automatically assuming that it will lead you to fulfilment. Find yourself, listen to your true inner voice, and move forward in response to its promptings.

look to your future

EXERCISE THREE

Your ancestors had dreams for the future, especially if they were immigrants; and some of your imprinting may include this sense of aspiration. You can focus on this and tap into its power—even if your own life goals are very different. How do you see your truly fulfilled self? This exercise will help you to believe in that vision.

1. ***Take a trip to the future.*** *Visualize your future self at some moment of achievement—such as having your first novel accepted by an agent or publisher, or being thanked for your work on behalf of an underprivileged group. Bask for one minute in that vision. Why should you not succeed?*
2. ***Revisit past achievements.*** *Think of all the achievements you have notched up since childhood, the skills you have acquired. Since then you have chosen a particular course. What makes you think you cannot branch out in the direction of your dream?*
3. ***Project your potential.*** *Returning to your vision of future achievement, think of it as a motivating symbol. Life won't be exactly as you imagine it. But if you follow your motivation and believe in it, the future that is right for you will happen.*

decide what to change

Change occurs only after a decision has been made. The decision to change can occur in an instant, but usually comes only after a choice becomes clear. To reveal the possibilities, take time to listen to your heart as well as your head, identify what does not feel right about your life and what you want to be different, and write down your findings.

For this purpose, and to help you with the exercises in this book, buy a blank notebook—this will be your "power thinking journal". Whatever you choose to write in your journal, make sure that it is true for you. After all, changing the way you think is one of the most significant steps you can take in life. This is a great way to process and clarify your feelings and goals, and to express unarticulated thoughts.

Changes are not only possible and predictable, but to deny them is to be an accomplice to one's own unnecessary vegetation.

GAIL SHEEHY, AMERICAN WRITER, SOCIAL CRITIC

Keep your journal safe and in an accessible place, such as your "think tank" (see p.34). Make time to write up your entries; this could be a daily power practice (see p.48) or something you do less frequently but still regularly. Each session might last a certain length of time, say 15 or 30 minutes; or you might write a minimum amount at every session, say half a page or a page. Whenever you write, do so in the belief that whatever you need to discover will be revealed to you on the page. Develop a freeflowing style. Do not worry about grammar, punctuation or spelling. Do not edit your words. You do not even have to be sure that you are writing the truth—indeed, you do not even have to make sense! The important thing is that you are expressing yourself. As long as you are doing this, sense, truth and clarity will come over time.

six steps to change

EXERCISE FOUR

Here are six steps that can help you acknowledge what it is you want to change. Go through each step in your power thinking journal. Make these changes come alive.

1. **Make a "more" list.** *List the things you already have in your life that you want more of: meditation, spy novels, sex, sports, or time to chill with a beer? Do not judge or edit your ideas. Wanting to enjoy your life does not make you greedy or hedonistic.*
2. **Make a "want" list.** *List the things you don't have that you want, from inner peace to ivory curtains to invisible braces. Again, do not judge or edit your thoughts.*
3. **Make a "fantasy changes" list.** *List all the things you would change in your life if you knew that it was possible. Do not be concerned how far-fetched your ideas might be.*
4. **Engage "ponder power".** *Review your lists. What stands out? What are you instinctively drawn to focus on? What changes are just crying out to be made?*
5. **Choose and decide.** *Choose what you want to change and decide to change it—even if you do not yet know how. Making the decision is a powerful first step in itself.*
6. **Stay connected.** *Keep change at the forefront of your mind by reviewing your lists daily. Add and delete things. Change will happen more easily and quickly than you anticipate if you focus and refocus on what you have written down.*

centres of power

When training in the gym to build up part of your body, you use a particular technique to isolate the selected area. You strengthen this area through many repetitions of the technique. Our whole lives are like our physical bodies—we all have parts that are already strong ("centres of power") and parts we want to strengthen ("challenge areas").

Our centres of power are those aspects of our lives where we feel competent, confident, fulfilled, at ease and truly alive, where we get results. Our challenge areas are aspects where we experience dissatisfaction or even frustration, where we seem to lack answers, where we do not get good results. We avoid our challenge areas because they make us feel inadequate, incompetent, sometimes even unlovable.

It is important to identify your centres of power and challenge areas. If your challenge areas are neglected for too long they can debilitate your centres of power—just as when your health is neglected, your career, home and other areas of life also suffer.

If you want to convert your challenge areas into centres of power, you must be prepared to experience a degree of discomfort. For example, if you are overweight, the idea of going to the gym can be hugely intimidating. To face any physical and social discomfort involved, concentrate on avoiding the common pitfall of undervaluing the future. We are told so often to live in the present that future gains can seem very remote. But remember: the future will happen. The gains you are working for *will* materialize.

Look at the following key areas of your life. Which are your power centres and which are your challenge areas? For each category, ask yourself: do I give this area the attention it deserves?

CAREER A person with a strong career power centre is content with their professional development and experiences high job satisfaction. Challenges come from confidence anxieties, overwork, or a sense of being undervalued or in a job that seems unimportant, tedious or demanding.

SIGNIFICANT RELATIONSHIP Love, emotional support, physical contact and good company are obvious blessings. The challenge can come from finding a suitable partner in the first place, or making the relationship fulfilling if you have already have a partner.

FRIENDS AND FAMILY When friends and family are a power centre, you feel emotional connection, support, understanding, trust, and enjoy social interaction. Challenges can arise from feuds, betrayal, poor communication, or emotions such as jealousy or resentment.

RECREATION AND REJUVENATION Recreation is not only something for your annual vacation. It helps to have ways to relax and have fun all year round on a regular basis. Best of all is to do something that is enjoyable, social and healthy. The challenge might be to find people who share your interests, whether it is scuba diving, mountain climbing going to the opera, or in-depth discussions about books or movies; or it might be discovering a new activity that you find fulfilling.

PHYSICAL ENVIRONMENT Neglecting your surroundings—home, garden, car, office, wardrobe—can affect your mood and self-esteem. Pride in your environment is a strength. A sense of domestic chaos only just held at bay is a sign that a key part of your life—your relationship with your environment—needs attention.

HEALTH AND FITNESS Your diet, your weight, your vitality—these are important not only to you, but also those close to you. Being proactive in looking after yourself ideally includes a healthy, active lifestyle combined with good general health knowledge and regular medical check-ups. The challenge might be lack of exercise, poor diet, or various addictions (caffeine, alcohol, painkillers, and so on).

We don't see things as they are, we see things as we are.

ANAÏS NIN, FRENCH WRITER

PERSONAL DEVELOPMENT Life is not only for living, it is also for growing. The happiest people keep their mind learning, their soul searching and their spirit shining. In this sphere the challenge might be to overcome directionlessness, to face up to past disappointments and learn from them, or to adapt your goals to changing circumstances.

FINANCES Good money management (or debt management) is no less important than having a good income. The healthy approach is to make money work for you, and be aware of both risks and opportunities. The unhealthy approach is to be inefficient about bills and record-keeping, and to see money as an unpredictable element, like rain.

SPIRITUALITY Your spirituality is your sense of connection to a higher power: the spirit, God, the universe, or whatever else you believe in. It is good to try to put into words what you believe. If you experience merely a hopeless void, this is a challenge area that needs attention.

build your centres of power

EXERCISE FIVE

You've made a vow to yourself to be proactive. It's time to put that intention into practice. If you desire for something to change in your life, isn't it foolish to be inactive?

1. ***In your power thinking journal write down*** *the current state of each of your key life areas. Ask yourself which are the challenge areas that cause you the most unease, frustration and/or stress.*
2. ***Pick one challenge area*** *you feel compelled to do something about—an aspect of your life on which you are willing to focus attention in order to turn things around.*
3. ***Write down every aspect*** *that gives you trouble within that challenge area. For example, if the challenge area is finances, maybe you feel it is difficult to control your monthly spending; and you are always late paying bills; and you feel too uncomfortable and ignorant to talk to a financial professional.*
4. ***Choose one aspect*** *of your challenge area and start to work on it. (For example, you might start reading up on the technical terms you know financial advisors use.) That done, return to your list and start on another aspect. Continue until you feel you have turned this challenge area into a centre of power. One step at a time will get you there.*

feel different, feel better

If you are out of touch with your emotions, you could be sad, distressed or nervous and not even know it. You could easily say and do things that do not serve you, find it difficult to make decisions and not even know why. To assist you in developing a higher degree of emotional self-awareness, check in with your feelings throughout the day. Start by taking a deep breath. Then take a moment to ask yourself how you feel right now. If an answer does not appear immediately, take another deep breath and ask the question again. Usually the answer will come to mind. If it does not, take out your power thinking journal and try to express in writing how you feel. Awareness of your feelings allows you to be more present to yourself and to others. Then, in the broadest terms, you have two options: you can either clear or adjust your feelings in some way; or you can take action to make yourself feel better. In practice the appropriate response is often a mixture of the two.

Do not judge yourself for your feelings. They will always be valid. If you discover that you are envious or jealous or irritated, that is perfectly understandable. Simply notice how you feel, and think about the underlying cause. This might run deeper than you at first imagine. That is why arguments flare up over quite trivial concerns: there is usually some deeper reason, perhaps a resentment that, as you perceive it, you are always being told what to do, or that the other person always thinks they know best. Try to dig to the roots of your emotions.

When we become aware of our feelings and acknowledge them without judgment, we can let them go and get on with living. If a friend has forgotten your birthday, any hurt you might harbour is only going to strain your relationship with them. You have a choice about what you do with your feelings. Sometimes the best choice is simply to acknowledge them and let them go. Or you can take considered action—in which case your feelings have served the purpose of energizing you, and again are ready to be let go.

When you let disappointment or frustration turn into your reason for not pursuing a goal, or when you act rashly in the heat of the moment, your feelings are ruling you. Learn instead to rule them. Stand back to let them have their say. But don't let them monopolize your attention. Their function is to help, not to hinder. When you want to feel better, acknowledge your emotions and ask yourself compassionately, "What are you going to do about it?" Listen for the answer and begin.

a space to grow

When you were young, maybe you built a tree house, or played in a doll house or adapted the crawl-space under the back porch into your own private hideaway. This was a place you went to play, to think and to spend some quality time alone.

Throughout the ages people have created places in their living or working environments to serve specific functions—the bedroom for sleeping, the kitchen for cooking, the den for pool playing, the meditation room for reflection, the study for working or reading, and so on. Every activity that is important to us deserves its own dedicated place, and the same goes for power thinking. So I call on you now to set aside a special space—even a small part of a room—where the primary function is power thinking. This place is your "think tank". It is where you go to grow, to plan, a place where you work on moving forward.

I go into the wilderness and rediscover the home within.

CHINA GALLAND, AMERICAN WRITER, NATURALIST

The sole purposes of this power thinking space will be creation and contemplation. It will be a quiet and a private place. The walls of your think tank might be lined with your diplomas to remind you of past achievements, or you might put up a poster of a favourite figure, such as Albert Einstein or Martin Luther King, or a physical representation of your goal or ambition (see p.79). Or you might prefer nothing on the wall aside from inspirational quotes. When you are facing a challenge, solving a problem or deciding on a course of action, these images or sayings will remind you of who you are. Be grounded by them as you listen to your intuition and call on your inner wisdom and strength.

create your think tank

EXERCISE SIX

The following steps will help you to create your think tank—your personal power thinking space where you go to develop the master plan for your life.

1. ***Where will my think tank be?*** *Any quiet and private place—your office at home or work, a closet, garage, attic, porch—even a desk or an enclosed corner of a room.*
2. ***Keep some items in your think tank*** *that can support your creative thinking. As well as your power thinking journal, they might include a few books or inspirational objects.*
3. ***Make your think tank your personal sanctuary.*** *Use it for planning, exploring creative solutions, research, rest, and rejuvenating entertainment. The exercises in this book are ideal think tank activities. Do not use your think tank for paying bills, watching TV—or anything else that does not honour the purpose of this special place.*
4. ***Set aside think tank time.*** *Decide how much daily or weekly time you will devote to your think tank, and stick to this resolution.*

from thinking to action

The folk singer Joan Baez said: "Action is the antidote to despair." Whatever ails you or whenever you are feeling unfulfilled in your life, action is the right antidote—even if your action is sitting on a park bench and listening to what your soul has to say.

> *Start by doing what is necessary, then do what is possible, and suddenly you are doing the impossible.*
>
> SAINT FRANCIS OF ASSISI, ITALIAN MONK

Usually we do not take action because we think it will be less painful to do nothing. You might stay home from a party because even though you want to go and have fun, you won't know many people there and think no one will talk to you, or you might see your ex there with a new partner. This situation reflects a common inherent thinking pattern in which we project negative outcomes, always anticipating that things will turn out badly, that the consequences we seek will not occur.

The solution is action. Very often our expectations of a negative outcome are based on ungrounded fears, not genuine knowledge. The more you overcome your reluctance and take action, the more you will realize just how often things can go well for you. Before long you will switch from projecting negative outcomes to projecting positive ones.

What are the situations in your life where your fears and uncertainties have stopped you from taking action? Have you stayed with an unsuitable partner because you feel that being alone will be worse, or that you will not find anyone better? Have you been unable to start an exercise program because you think you will not be able to keep it up? Identify where you have chosen inaction because you cannot see things going well. Then begin to take action to prove yourself wrong.

release burdening thoughts

EXERCISE SEVEN

The way you think either serves you or sabotages you. Begin to recognize and eliminate thoughts and beliefs you have about yourself and your life that are keeping you from taking action, experiencing happiness and realizing what you want to create.

1. ***Write down*** *your main dreams and goals, the things you want to create in your life, the positive experiences you would like to see happen.*
2. ***On another sheet of paper,*** *write down all the sabotaging thoughts or beliefs that block your progress, such as "I am too old to do that" or "No one will want me" or "I won't be any good at that so why even try?" Take a deep breath and keep writing, without editing, what comes to mind for three minutes, or until you feel these negative ideas are all out of your system. Then take a deep breath and see if there are any more.*
3. ***Once you feel they are all out,*** *read them out loud to yourself. Precede each negative thought with this phrase: "I release the following self-sabotaging thought and belief from my life." As you say the thought, feel yourself letting it go.*
4. ***When you are done,*** *destroy the paper you wrote your negative thoughts on. Tear it to shreds, throw it on the fire. As you do so, focus again on releasing these unserving ideas from your life. Your dreams and goals remain—now free from their shackles.*

choose where to begin

CHAPTER TWO

No doubt you have often heard people say, "I have figured it all out in my mind?" The mind is our most powerful tool in creating what we want—and yet our mind power cannot help unless we combine it with action.

There is an Irish proverb: you never plough a field by turning it over in your mind. Thinking about our lives and the changes we would like to make is only the beginning. Taking action is where the magic happens, where results happen, where the proof that you had it all right—or wrong—in your mind is revealed.

This power thinking adventure is largely about combining your mind power with specific actions to create a new perspective, to take a step forward that may very well move your life in a whole new direction. Whatever it is you desire, I invite you to get your power thinking journal and a pen to write with, and schedule yourself some time to get clear about what you want to create. Then carve out some more time to take the action necessary to make your desires real.

change starts with intention

To ring in the new millennium I went to Machu Picchu, the famous mountain stronghold in Peru, considered by many to be one of the most sacred places on Earth. Here I spent the week with several shamans, priest-like wise people who wore vibrant multicoloured robes and smiled serenely. Shamans perform rituals and share their wisdom with you in vague and visionary language, making it necessary for you to give a lot of thought to what their words mean and how they relate to your personal situation.

Things do change—if you let them.

PATRICIA MACLACHLAN, AMERICAN WRITER

Shamans guide many people on their life path. But you will never hear a shaman say that you need to "create an action plan" or "write a strategy" for your life. Instead shamans talk about "intention". An intention is an aim, a desire, something you want to see materialize. Shamans use rituals to assist you in "setting" an intention.

ritualize your intentions

There are many ways to "set" an intention. You could **stand on a mountain top** and profess your resolution to the trees and sky around you. You could **write down** some negative thing you want to release from your life on a piece of paper, go to the beach and **bury it**. You could **wash your hands** in a basin to affirm your intention of rinsing loneliness from your life. Or you could **light a candle** to support your intention of achieving more inner peace. Intention is powerful in itself. It is a way of proclaiming to yourself and to the universe that you are committed to change and renewal. Think of an important intention now and affirm it.

Intention allows you to focus on bringing something into your life even if you do not know how that will be possible. Perhaps you desire a soulmate, or a new direction in your career, or a cure for an illness. When you set a strong intention you begin to move toward your desire. You do this by activating your psyche—and the energy of the universe itself—to support you in your quest.

In Peru, at a communal ritual, there comes a point when you are handed three coca leaves. You bring them to your lips and blow on them as if breathing your intentions into them. Then you present the three leaves to other people in your community, and they blow on them in the same way and pass them on. You are given many other leaves and pass them on in the same way. It is as if you are giving birth to your intentions, and sending them out into the world to be created.

You can, of course, think up your own personal ritual as a way to manifest your intentions. Some suggestions to set you off in the right direction are given in the box opposite.

how do you act?

Thinking is what our mind does to figure out our lives, our relationships, our plans, and the world around us. All the activities of the mind—thinking, planning, choosing, deciding—need to be followed up with action. Thinking without action is like a recipe without a cook.

Let us live, while we are alive!

JOHANN WOLFGANG VON GOETHE, GERMAN WRITER, PHILOSOPHER

There are two categories of action. Action freely chosen and intentionally implemented is called proaction; action taken in response to some outside factor is called reaction. It should also be said that there is a third type, inaction, or passivity, when you take no action at all.

In other words, proaction is when you make things happen, and reaction is when you let things happen to you. Usually, in being reactive, you do not do a lot of thinking beforehand. This can lead to frustration, depression, damaged relationships, a sense of your life being out of your control, and other negative consequences.

There will certainly be areas in your life where you are naturally more proactive and other areas where you are more reactive. For example, you might tend to be reactive with your family—a casual, ill-considered remark from a sibling can make you reply without thinking, and even start you off on a tirade. But you might be proactive with your career—always thinking three steps ahead, considering what needs to be done next, anticipating difficulties before they arise.

Whenever you hear yourself complaining about something, recognize this as an opportunity to move from reaction to proaction. For example, if you are single and you complain about how you never seem

proactive quiz

EXERCISE EIGHT

Complete this quiz to find out if you are proactive, reactive or inactive.

1. *At a family gathering you see someone you don't know. Do you:* ***A.*** *Walk up and introduce yourself to ascertain their connection to your family?* ***B.*** *Ask someone else who they are?* ***C.*** *Try to overhear the information by eavesdropping on their conversation?*

2. *Your new paper boy has been leaving your newspaper in the wrong place all week. Do you:* ***A.*** *Catch him on his next round and let him know your preference?* ***B.*** *Complain about him to your neighbours?* ***C.*** *Do nothing in the hope that he'll improve?*

3. *After three dates with someone, you decide you don't want to pursue a relationship. When they next call, do you:* ***A.*** *Thank them for the dates, but tell them you do not want to pursue a relationship?* ***B.*** *Lyingly say that you got back together with your ex?* ***C.*** *Not return their phone call—or any subsequent calls?*

If you answered ***A*** each time you are generally proactive; if ***B*** you are reactive; and if ***C*** you are inactive—and it would really serve you to work on being more proactive.

to meet anyone who might make a great partner for you, ask yourself how you can be proactive to change this situation. Only when you ask the question will the answer appear. You could tell all your married friends that you are looking for someone and ask them to fix you up with single people they know. You could ask someone you like at work out on a date. You could smile at people at the gym, enrol in a night class, or join a new social group of some kind. Or you could place an ad in the paper, or on the internet. You could also, of course, *reply* to such an ad, and this course of action would be on the borderline where the reactive and proactive become somewhat blurred; but on balance this would still be proactive behaviour, because it would involve breaking out of your habitual circumstances and taking a leap into the unknown.

hats off to proaction!

In America in 1896 it was fashionable for women to wear wide-brimmed hats displaying stuffed woodpeckers, owls, or exotic birds. One popular style was a dozen small, colourful birds in a circle going all the way around the hat. Many of the species of birds used to decorate the hats were on the verge of extinction. This carnage outraged two Boston women, Harriet Hemenway and Minna Hall, who were suffragists already busy working hard to win women's right to vote. Harriet and Minna got proactive. They educated the people of Boston, raised money, lobbied politicians and founded the Massachusetts Audubon Society, whose purpose was—and is—to protect birds. Harriet and Minna were largely responsible for the passage of laws in 1903 that prohibited milliners from selling or possessing the feathers of various birds.

When you are proactive a wealth of new experiences open up before you like a promised land. By committing to this way of thinking you take a massive step toward achieving the life you desire for yourself. Proactive people don't accept things the way they are—they take action to make them the way they want them to be. By adopting a healthy, proactive lifestyle you can add years to your life; and add life to your years.

Proaction does not preclude being responsive to circumstances. On the contrary, it will often involve coming to a swift understanding of circumstances as they evolve, seeing opportunities to make a positive impact, and seizing those opportunities in a timely fashion. Timely in this context does not mean hasty: remember that premature responses are characteristic of reactiveness, not proactiveness.

It is worth taking stock of how proactive you are about key areas of life. Have you chosen your job or has your job chosen you? Try making appropriate adjustments to this basic formula of self-questioning to probe other dimensions of your life—your home, your friends, the way you spend your weekends and vacations, and so on. Also, think about the way you are with other people: do you tend to go along with what they say, or do you find yourself readily taking initiatives? Some people find it hard to contribute crisply to shared decision-making. We all know what it feels like to stand in a group, waiting for someone to make a firm decision about where to go next. Being proactive means having ideas and acting on them—whether solo or working cooperatively and constructively with others.

eliminate catastrophic thinking

Often we don't take action because we consider only dramatic solutions and fail to recognize simpler or more effective options. This is catastrophic thinking. Karen loved her job as an auditor of college programs in her county, but an old back injury caused her pain on her long drives to the various far-flung schools. As a catastrophic thinker, Karen initially decided that the only way to be free of pain was to quit her job.

Catastrophic thinkers project that if they gain one thing, they have to lose something else. Adjust that perspective. Instead of asking "What do I have to give up to gain what I want?" you can ask a better question: "How can I create what I want without giving up what I have?"

Change your thoughts and you change your world.

NORMAN VINCENT PEALE, AMERICAN METHODIST LEADER, WRITER

This is what Karen did in the end. She considered other possibilities. Instead of driving home every night, she could cut her hours in the car by going out on the road for a few days at a time and sleeping in motels. She could carry out audits for some of the most distant colleges electronically, reviewing data and conducting interviews by phone, while a colleague could do the site inspections. In fact, Karen's consideration of other options led her to recognize that what she really loved about her job was helping colleges become more effective in the delivery of their programs, and that she could do this by becoming a consultant on site at the colleges in her area. Through eliminating catastrophic thinking, Karen did not simply make her old job more workable: she discovered a new focus in her job that made her even happier.

There are certainly times when you have been a catastrophic thinker. Often we think this way when confronted with situations that are crucially important to us, because we are emotionally involved and cannot see all the possible ways through. Approach such problems in a positive spirit, knowing that the most extreme remedy—the one in which you lose as much as you gain—is unlikely to be the best. Catastrophes are usually like nightmares—their terror lies only in the imagination.

nurture the soil of self

In our rushed world we can easily find ourselves devoting all our attention to the daily tasks of maintaining our home, our job and our relationships with others. Often we forget to attend to our most important relationship—with ourselves. Our souls need soothing after bombardment by unrelaxing, distressing or disappointing situations.

You might think of yourself as an action person, someone full of energy, averse to passive self-indulgence. Forget this kind of thinking. Inaction is not self-indulgent if conducted in the right frame of mind. We all need to find a way to disengage from the outside pressures of our lives for a time and connect with our own inner sanctuary, the serene, quiet place at the centre of our being. Devise what I call a "daily power practice" for yourself: the energizing vocabulary will remind you that you are doing something truly constructive, however low-key it might seem. At home or work, spend time in your think tank, just thinking, meditating, writing your power thinking journal or making positive affirmations. Or your daily power practice might be a combination of spiritual contemplation and physical movement, such as yoga, qigong or t'ai chi.

Sometimes a life, like a house, needs renovating, the smell of new wood, new rooms in the heart, unimagined until one begins the work.

DORIS SCHWERIN, AMERICAN WRITER

Other ideas for a daily power practice include chanting, singing, stretching, swimming, walking on the beach, taking your dog for a walk, or simply feeding the ducks in the park. If some of these things strike you as mundane or clichéed, adjust your perspective: commonplace pleasures are not automatically inferior.

clear the field

EXERCISE NINE

The daily power practice is a great way to clear the inner spaces of your mind. You can enhance its effects by also clearing out the physical spaces in your life. Like most people, you probably hang on to stuff—too much stuff. Hanging on to old stuff is a way of clinging to a past that is gone and best released. Follow these steps for eliminating the clutter in your life. You will free up space not only in your home but also in your mind—releasing more energy for focusing on new ideas and what is ahead.

1. ***Release past relationships.*** *Throw away gifts, letters and photos of past loves. If you wish, just keep a couple of mementoes, reminders of special times. Let your past relationships occupy as little space in your home as they do in your mind and your heart.*
2. ***Clear your closets.*** *Get rid of old clothes, old sports equipment, gadgets that are broken and out-of date, and projects started and long abandoned.*
3. ***Eliminate information overload.*** *Get rid of all the excess information in your home, in your car and on your computer. Throw out bills, receipts and financial information you no longer need. Dump piles of old magazines and other mail more than 6 months old.*
4. ***Do a final sweep*** *throughout your home while asking yourself, "What could I beneficially release from my life?"*

power thinking fitness

CHAPTER THREE

In an instant you can opt to begin a fitness program or a healthy eating plan. In the same way, you can choose in an instant to be a power thinker.

We all know that realizing a major ambition is not something you can do in the time it takes you to think up that ambition. You cannot in an instant turn your body into a specimen of optimal physical conditioning, or turn your mind into a model of optimal mental conditioning. It takes time to become the person that you envisage yourself as being, time in which you consistently and with conviction work at your power thinking exercises and take the decisive steps along your true course.

Power thinking is not simply a tool that anyone can immediately start to use in all life's situations. A fundamental part of being a power thinker is first understanding, or deciding upon, what you want. In this chapter we learn how to recognize and grasp ways to enhance our self-awareness; we explore new techniques for reflection and planning; and we discover one of the most useful tools in power thinking—goal-setting.

self-coaching

One day you are visited by an old high school friend. When the day starts, you are looking forward to reminiscing, catching up and having fun. But as the day progresses, your friend makes a critical comment every few minutes—you have become overweight, you really haven't done much with your life, you seem unhappy, you must be sickening for something because you seem rather lethargic, you just said the wrong thing to the waitress ... and so on. At the end of the day your friend declares that she wants to join you again tomorrow. Your heart sinks.

Words are, of course, the most powerful drug used by mankind.

RUDYARD KIPLING, ENGLISH AUTHOR, NOBEL PRIZE WINNER

I am guessing you would decide that another day with this "old chum" would be the end of you—and you would be right. Now here's the catch—you do have someone like this in your life, and if you look in the mirror you will see who I mean.

Unless you're firm right now and send away your internal "old chum", the companion will continue to visit—because this unfriendly and unsupportive old voice lives inside you, rarely challenged and rarely questioned. You are the one who beats yourself up all day when you have overslept and arrived late to work, or have neglected some trivial duty or chore, or have presumptuously entertained for a moment (heaven forbid!) a vision of self-transformation. You are the one you hang out with all day long, every day. As the day progresses do you build yourself up or knock yourself down? Do you feel confident, capable, fully equipped to realize your vision—or do you tell yourself something your "old chum" would say?

An early step on the way to power thinking is to rid yourself of this irritating companion—or to put it more accurately, to *change* this person who inhabits your consciousness, so that she—or he, of course, (I use "she" for clarity)—is fully supportive to you in the realization of your ambitions. This in turn requires you to understand how wrong this person has a habit of being. You may feel that she can offer lots of proof, beyond a shadow of a doubt, as to why your life and your psyche are screwed up, why you cannot do something, why this is as good as it can get for you. But if you acknowledge that power thinking is possible for all of us, and can lead to increased fulfilment, then it is easy for you to acknowledge how damaging are the mutterings of this doubter, who dampens your spirit whenever she shows up.

The question to hold in your mind every day, like a compass navigating you through life, is not "Why are things not working?" If you ask this, your doubter will certainly pipe up with a ready answer, making it clear where to lay the blame. Instead, ask yourself daily, "What do I want and how can I get it?"

Instead of wallowing in your past—the unfortunate circumstances, the bad timing, the setbacks—and finding there the blame for any current lack of accomplishment or fulfilment, look to the future. The present and the future are all you have; the past is long gone and cannot serve you any more. Start to be proactive and move toward making things happen—instead of letting things happen to you. Of course, you still have an inner companion, a shared self with whom you commune whenever you embark on any solitary thinking. Train that "old chum"

the power of POW!

A useful self-coaching tool is something I call your POW—your Personal Objective Word. This is a word or phrase you use to motivate yourself into action. You say it to yourself on waking and throughout the day to remind you of your objectives. My POW is "Avanti", the Italian for "Get going!" To me, the letters also represent "Apply valuable action now toward improvement." Other POWs could be "Go!" "Galvanize!" "Focus!" "Do It Now!" "I am alert, awake, alive!" Use one of these or create your own to motivate you and add energy to your day. You could sing it or accompany it by an action, like a "thumbs up"—anything to make its message more vivid.

to cheer you up, to believe in you, to remind you that you know deep down you are going to win. True, your inner companion has had access to all your previous thoughts and experiences, living alongside you for as long as you have been on the planet. But at the moment she is flawed in her judgments, because the only authority she recognizes is that of the past. You, who have understood but not yet practised the transformative wonders of power thinking, know that genuine authority lies in our potential for the future—and that such potential is infinite. Your companion is backward-sighted. Imagine yourself correcting her perceptions by supplying her with forward-sighted spectacles. There on the horizon, which was previously beyond the scope of her vision, is the future you, taking charge of your life and reaping the benefits of being focused, energetic and confident.

Coaching your inner companion—your alter ego, the person with whom you maintain a constant interior dialogue—to see what is possible for you both is a key step on the road to self-realization. In time a fusion will take place between the two different perspectives, as your inner companion starts to see as you do, and the discouraging comments become less and less frequent. Until this happens, think of yourself as a trainer, taking satisfaction from working with a promising yet out-of-condition student. All the negative voices come from this uneducated source inside your head. Draw upon your deep personal well of wisdom, your belief in a positive future, to silence the cautionary tales of precedent. Train your whole self to look forward and outward, and to know that what you see out there is reachable—as undoubtedly it is.

increase self-awareness

Do you regularly examine your life, your thoughts and your actions? We are creatures of habit. You may be doing something habitually that you no longer have reason to do, or holding on to thoughts that have long been disproved or no longer serve you. The only way to be true to yourself is to penetrate such layers of habit and live by a refreshed awareness of the self underneath.

Self-awareness means being clear about what you want, being able to articulate your vision, knowing your opinions, what you like and don't like, what you stand for and what you will not tolerate. Take some of the time you ordinarily spend getting to know other people, or learning about the world around you, and use it to get to know the only person you will always be with—yourself. Your relationship with yourself is the most important human relationship you have. It is through self-awareness and self-love that you can best give yourself to others.

To understand is hard. Once one understands, action is easy.

SUN YAT-SEN, CHINESE STATESMAN

To spend time thinking about who you are is not the narrow, circular, self-defining exercise some people might expect it to be. Far from being narrow, it is actually liberating. The better you know yourself, the more you will be able to trust, love and serve yourself for your own highest good and the highest good of the people and projects you choose to value. I have taught workshops where participants could not share with a small group of people one thing they liked about themselves, and could not say what their highest value was or what they wanted their life to be about. Life is not for sleepwalking—it is for

the ultimate questionnaire

EXERCISE TEN

If the idea of developing self-awareness seems a little difficult, start by taking out your power thinking journal and writing your answers to the following questions. They are intensely probing, and designed to deepen your self-awareness. If you don't have an answer to some of the questions, ponder them for a day, then return to write your answers later. Your first attempts will probably turn out to be drafts that you later choose to revise. Self-awareness always unfolds in this way—it is not a static subject, and only a long-term approach, not a still snapshot, can do justice to it.

1. *What purpose have you given to your life?*
2. *What are you passionate about?*
3. *What are you for and what are you against?*
4. *What do you really believe in?*
5. *What do you know to be true about you?*
6. *What do you struggle with and why?*
7. *What easily upsets you?*
8. *What do you long for?*

skipping, fully awake. If you do not choose a direction in life you will just keep on being blown about like a leaf in the wind, unable to see obstacles until you hit them.

All roads lead to Rome—or Katmandu, or Vancouver, or Venice. You cannot make a wrong turn once you are on the path to increased self-awareness. To turn my metaphor into an imagined fact, a journey to some distant significant place, such as Stonehenge, or Mecca, or Jerusalem, would certainly provide you with rich insights into yourself. If you do not have the inclination or the wherewithal for a pilgrimage, there are many other opportunities available to you for enhancing self-awareness where you are now.

Journal writing is a voyage to the interior.

CHRISTINA BALDWIN, AMERICAN WRITER

Some of these opportunities are presented to you in the form of exercises in this chapter. In addition to these, you might consider taking up or developing the practice of meditation, or perhaps a traditional mind-body-spirit practice, such as t'ai chi or yoga. Psychotherapy, counselling and one of the many 12-step programs (such as the one run by Alcoholics Anonymous) all involve other people in the process of increasing your own self-awareness, and one of these methods might be rewarding for you if you feel any inclination toward a more structured self-awareness solution. At least once in their life, everyone can benefit from paying someone to listen to them—it can be uniquely refreshing.

However, you do not need to spend time with a professional counsellor or therapist to determine what motivates you, what scares you, what are the issues in your life, and what approaches you might take to resolve those issues. You can increase your self-awareness unaided.

Approach the self-awareness challenge as if you were a researcher using yourself as a case study. Adopt an attitude of professional objectivity and do not judge your subject—yourself—for any choice you might make or decline. Allow yourself to notice things without judging yourself, without putting yourself "in the wrong". What is it that is preventing you from fulfilling the most profound ambitions you have set for yourself? What obstacles might you be putting in your own path? Try to make some acquaintance with whatever it is about yourself that blocks you—that gets in the way of your being more magnificent.

Although no one can go back and make a brand new start, anyone can start from now and make a brand new ending.

ANONYMOUS

The relevance of self-awareness to power thinking is clear and direct. Understanding is the best tool with which to break open an inner block. Its light is like a far-reaching lubricant that forces its way into seized-up hinges and makes their action free again.

We can take comfort from being centred so much within ourselves: this is our home, our refuge, where no-one can reach us. There is a stillness at the heart of our being that is invulnerable to external pressures, as long as we can remain in touch with that precious core. Yet however comfortable we find it being inside ourselves, it is healthy to break out from time to time and take a broader view. Set aside time for travelling beyond the self to see how we might look from a little farther off. This is a matter of seeing ourselves not through the eyes of others (that would be impossible), but through our own eyes, from a more distant viewpoint. Looking at ourselves along this fresh perspective, we may see routes to fulfilment that had previously escaped our notice.

develop intuition

Seeing, hearing, touching, smelling, tasting—we all know how our five senses perceive the world. But all of us have at least one more, an internal tool of perception—our intuition. Sometimes you might have a thought that you cannot justify in logical terms. For example, you might feel, as someone is talking, a physical sensation that makes you aware, despite the lack of evidence, that the truth is being withheld. Or maybe sometimes you act without thinking—perhaps reaching out to catch a falling object before your conscious mind even realizes what is happening. These are both examples of intuition, which comes either as instinctive thoughts in our mind or as visceral feelings in our body.

Intuition is a spiritual faculty and does not explain, but simply points the way.

FLORENCE SCOVEL SHINN, AMERICAN ILLUSTRATOR, METAPHYSICIST

Often when I have been coaching a client, a question has popped up in my head, sending the conversation to a deeper level and revealing a major challenge in the client's life—which would have gone unacknowledged if I had not asked that unprompted question.

The next time when you are talking to someone and a thought comes unbidden into your head, share it: say it. It may turn out to be the turning point of the conversation. You might say, "I have an unrelated thought I would like to bounce off you," or "I am having the sense that ...". In this way you will start to trust and use your intuition. Power thinking cannot depend on reason alone: it involves using your full toolkit of perception, and understanding that, just as emotion can distort our responses, intuition can sharpen them. Through intuition we increase our awareness of how we can best serve ourselves, and others.

use your sixth sense

EXERCISE ELEVEN

To develop your intuition, try an empathetic approach to conversations with people you are friendly with yet do not know very well. You might have such a conversation with a fellow guest at a party or someone you chat with at the coffee machine at work.

1. ***Focus entirely on the other person*** *as you talk. Stop any internal chatter in your head.*
2. ***Ask personal questions*** *that will elicit more than just a "yes" or "no". For example, "What challenges are you facing these days?" or "What are you looking forward to?" How well you know the person will determine the level of intimacy—remember to respect people's boundaries and their right to decline to answer.*
3. ***Listen between the lines*** *as the person responds. What are their body language and tone of voice telling you? Do you sense something that they are not saying?*
4. ***If you have an intuition,*** *consider sharing it. Express your ideas tactfully, as possibilities. For example, "Do I sense you might be worried about that?" is better than "You're worried about that, aren't you?"—which might make the person feel defensive.*
5. ***If your intuitive impressions were correct****—well done! Regardless of how accurate you are, if you offer your insights with a view to being of service to other people, they should be well received. Do this exercise in a spirit of compassion and magnanimity.*

challenge glamour and illusion

As an Epicurean, I love to peruse the dessert table at a buffet. Life, just like a dessert buffet, offers more choices than you can possibly have space for. In order to not waste your time and energy trying offerings that are better left alone, recognize two temptresses that can leave you powerless and deflated if you let them influence your actions: glamour and illusion.

If you keep adding little by little, it will soon become a heap.

HESIOD, ANCIENT GREEK POET

One leads to the other: seduced by glamour, we end up experiencing its promised sweetness turning sour, so that the initial appeal seems in retrospect to have been an illusion. Life, like a dessert, is all too often not what it appears to be. By anticipating that appearances can be deceptive, we learn to avoid some of the pitfalls that lie in wait for us on our quest. The superficial, the fake, are poisons often presented in a golden chalice. They may seem like unexpected windfalls, all the more welcome for taking us by surprise; or they may seem no less than what we deserve, or even part and parcel of our most cherished goals. Learning to identify the most dangerous kinds of allure is an important aspect of self-awareness. When we respond to a false stimulus, the blame can lie only with ourselves, for failing to understand what really matters to us—and allowing ourselves to respond, for a while, to something that matters not at all. Glamour and illusion qualify to be among the first targets of any power thinking purge.

I have a friend in Italy who for a long time was a journalist. Last year he opened a restaurant, a dream that had nagged him for years. Last year he also closed his restaurant. He found out that owning a restaurant is not a life of leisurely conversation with amusing people who compliment one's cuisine over white table linen and rare bottles of wine. That illusion was shattered once he realized that he had to be there every day, that not all customers are pleasant, that a restaurant kitchen is very hot, that when a waiter falls sick you have to wait tables yourself.

However, the experience also reminded him why he had loved being a journalist. The job had allowed him to get out and about, working on different projects, learning about all kinds of new things, meeting really fascinating people, and informing the public. Now he knows. The glamour is gone, the illusion exploded. What remains is a greater appreciation of the sweet reality of his life.

When glamour beckons, move forward—in a spirit of inquiry. Is it the real thing or a mirage? Do not give automatic value to whatever is deemed "cool" by others—even something like downsizing, which, whatever its virtues, cannot be right for everyone. Trust your intuition as you investigate. Distinguish true from false dawns.

pick your priorities

Four years ago Bert and his wife stood at the edge of a road overlooking five dry, barren acres he had recently purchased on the coast of northern California. He turned to her and said with conviction, "Honey, this is where our dream house will one day stand." And indeed it did, although Bert—a software engineer—knew nothing about building, and his job kept him busy all week. He knew that if he took things slowly and invested one day every weekend, and extra time when he could find it, eventually he and his wife would have their house. Step by step, one thing at a time, you can build or create whatever you want.

To achieve a dream in this way requires you to abandon the illusion that every day is a showcase for you to notch up another achievement. This is the Superman or Superwoman myth, as fictitious as the movie characters from whom these names are borrowed. Let go of any intention to deliver peak performance on a daily basis, and instead focus on optimal living. Having decided on your priorities in life, realize that progress usually comes step by step—not all at once. As you move toward your prioritized goals, you can enjoy a daily experience of life that is productive and fulfilling. You can take satisfaction from the knowledge that you are set upon your true

course—although this does not mean that every day you will be able to look back and see that the features of landscape have shifted.

You cannot enjoy optimal living while giving one hundred percent of your attention to each area of your life simultaneously, every waking hour, seven days a week. As a power thinker, you are proactive—but only, at any one time, in those areas of life that you have chosen to prioritize. Right now, consider the different sectors of your life (see pp.28–30), and isolate which ones will be your priority areas for the next three months, or six months, or a year—or whatever time frame you decide. Priority areas are aspects of your life where you want to see real change. If you want to move house, then "physical environment" would be a priority area, as it was for Bert. If you want to find a partner, or to improve or change your current partnership, "significant relationship" would be a priority area. Limit your priority areas to three and make sure that at least one is a "challenge area" (see p.28). Picking only three does not mean neglecting other areas, only that the priority areas will be in the spotlight and will receive most of your attention in terms of thinking, planning, resources and action.

Pick your three priority areas *before* setting specific intentions or goals. In your priority areas you can set big, bold intentions; in other areas you can make your goals more modest. Do not overdo things. You need energy in reserve to deal with unexpected situations and opportunities. Be realistic and be relaxed. Do not push yourself: pace yourself.

frame your ambition

> *Where the willingness is great, the difficulties cannot be great.*
>
> NICCOLÒ MACHIAVELLI, ITALIAN RENAISSANCE AUTHOR, STATESMAN

There are many different words related to our specific ambitions in life. We can have a goal, a target, a dream, a vision. The associations vary from term to term. Goal, which is perhaps overused these days, implies a particular aim that is achieved by determined effort. A target is like a goal, but is usually more specialized still. A dream and a vision are both impressively broad, but also imply a possible lack of realism—and might be deemed too grand for many commonplace ambitions. Perhaps ambition, despite its professional connotations, is the right word after all for our desire for self-improvement in a specific area of life: "ambitious" to go ballooning, suggests a degree of emotional commitment, and a willingness to apply effort, that the other words lack.

In formulating your ambition, follow this power-positive procedure designed to give you the best possible chance of success:

1. Write down your ambition. Your mind is a very powerful instrument, yet good things are many times more likely to happen if you commit them to writing. Get your ambitions out of your head and into your life by writing them in your power thinking journal or your personal planner, typing them into your computer, or tapping them into your hand-held electronic organizer.

2. Make yourself clear. Be sure to state your ambition clearly and concisely. Ask yourself, "If I lost this piece of paper and then found it again in a year's time, have I put down enough information or written clearly enough to remind me of exactly what I meant?" If you decide that you haven't, be as specific as you can. For example, "I would like a better job" would be too vague. It would be much clearer to write: "I would like to get a job that gave me greater responsibility with a company that treats employees well and whose mission I can be proud of."

3. Calibrate your ambition. Ask yourself what specific achievements will allow you to claim that your ambition has been realized. You need some kind of graduated scale to indicate to yourself when something has been accomplished. For example, it helps to be able to say, not "I want to do a course in woodworking," but "I want to do a course in woodworking so that I become skilled enough to make a kitchen table."

4. Keep your ambition realistic. Ask yourself if this is something that it is really possible to accomplish, bearing in mind your priorities and the circumstances of your life. If so, begin; if not, perhaps bring the horizon a little closer to where you are now. For example, instead of writing "I want to buy a new car," you might scale that back to "I want to save $5,000 toward a downpayment on a new car." It is fine, when devising an ambition, to allow for an element of good fortune. Although the most realistic ambitions eliminate risk altogether, risk-taking can be a key factor in realizing by power thinking a cherished ambition. Power thinking is most successful when allied with effort and potential—any risks must be entered into with full awareness.

5. Give your ambition a time frame. Setting a time frame does not mean abandoning your ambition if you fail to realize it on time. However, a time frame can work against the tendency many people have to keep their vision (that word again) marooned in a perpetual future. An ambition endlessly deferred is no ambition at all, merely a pipedream. Some people use ambition in this way to make themselves more interesting: "I'm planning to write a novel," they might say, or "I'm planning to learn astanga yoga." Make this resolution to yourself: do not allow an ambition any space in your head if after six months you have taken not a single step toward realizing it. Often the first step is to gather the relevant information. Do this without delay: an ill-informed ambition is no more than a gleam in your eye.

There remain some questions. What is the scale of this ambition we are talking about? And is it feasible to entertain two ambitions, or three, or even more? Neither of these questions can, in fact, be answered prescriptively, as we all differ in what we want to achieve. Moreover, the two issues are related to each other. It is not possible to say that a large ambition will leave no room for smaller ambitions. What about the person who is starting two projects with a view to only seeing one of them—the more promising—to a conclusion? We are all different; and you have to choose what will work best for you.

create an action plan

EXERCISE TWELVE

Once you have identified an ambition, write an action plan to identify all the steps you need to take—some simple, requiring only a few moments, others more challenging, requiring a few months. Make a plan for each of your priority areas.

1. ***Do you have all the information*** *you need about your ambition? If not, that is your first action. For example, if you want to buy a new home, have you found an area you'd like to move to and checked out house prices there? Or, if you want to switch careers, have you found out all you can about the vocations that attract you?*
2. ***Write out all the actions*** *you think you will need to take to fulfil your ambition in the order that is most appropriate for its realization. Be prepared to modify these steps in the light of new information or of circumstances as they develop.*
3. ***Set aside time*** *in your schedule planner to begin work on some of these actions.*
4. ***Review your ambition and your action plan daily,*** *in the morning and in the evening, to remind you of what you are working on—so that your conscious and subconscious minds can continue to work for you at all times.*
5. ***Identify any inner barriers*** *to the realization of your ambition (see pp.74–5).*
6. ***Refine your action plan continuously.*** *As time passes and you work through your plan, your ambition will probably become clearer—or may change altogether.*

the path of self-devotion

There will be days when your actions flow with ease, like ice cream in summer—and there will be days when every step feels like pushing an ice truck up a hill. On those difficult days you will require more of yourself to make things happen. You will have to call on your inner strength and personal commitment to move forward.

The trouble is, if you don't risk anything, you risk even more.

ERICA JONG, AMERICAN WRITER

Lisa was a young corporate executive. She loved her work, although it meant living much of her life on planes and in hotel rooms. One day, during a long flight delay, she came upon an art exhibition inside the airport, with rows of bright pictures painted by schoolchildren. As she looked at each one, she felt happy—remembering how much she herself loved to paint and how long it had been since she had lifted a brush. In that moment she made a choice—to be a painter once again.

Her action plan included taking classes on Saturdays, getting up even earlier than usual three days a week to get in some painting time, and taking her sketchbook around with her, even on work trips. She stuck with her plan and eventually found a way to do less travelling and devote more time to her art.

What about those Saturdays fighting off jetlag, or those early mornings when she wanted to sleep in—how did she get to her easel and palette? You might say it was her burning desire that got her going. On some days, you might be right. On other days, you might say it was "self-discipline", and you might also be right. Here, I present a new idea I want you to entertain: self-devotion.

What we call self-discipline is what gets you to do the things that are not necessarily gratifying, that you know you have to do, to prevent serious consequences from following. It is what makes us do the dirty dishes or mow the lawn; and it keeps a reformed drinker off the alcohol and the person with a heart condition off the cream cakes.

Self-devotion is an enhanced, proactive version of self-discipline. It is what we call on when we remind ourselves that, although we do not feel like doing this right now, it is time to take action in the service of our desires. Self-discipline is about unwillingness, forcing yourself to do something reluctantly. Self-devotion is about willingness—choosing to do something, even when you don't feel like it, in service to yourself. Be devoted to the realization of your desires and ambitions.

This will not always be easy. There will be days, after a disappointment, when you will want to pull the covers over your head and shoo away the world. There will be days when you doubt that you will be able to further your desires. There will be days when you will even doubt your desires. That's OK, normal, natural. As we move along our chosen path, we grow and metamorphose, becoming more purposeful—although sometimes, especially after a setback or a low self-esteem day, we can feel estranged from our purposes, in which case we have to choose to reacquaint ourselves with them.

Self-devotion—living from day to day with your desires held clearly in focus—is not for the faint of heart nor for the faint of faith in themselves. Earlier (p.64) I spoke of the importance of not pushing yourself, of not attempting to be Superman or Superwoman: this can be a recipe for burn-out. Still, know that following a path of self-devotion does involve a willingness to continue at times beyond the point at which you are inclined to stop. This sounds like pushing myself, you might interject. True, yet it is pushing yourself *with* rather than *against* the grain of your deepest motivation. It is like pushing a mechanical toy car that has stalled—one nudge and it trundles on its way again. We push ourselves not as a way of life, but to jolt ourselves into our natural forward rhythm. Soon this will feel right for us. It is the rhythm of our self-realization, which in due course will become as natural as breathing.

The only real risk is the risk of thinking too small.

FRANCES MOORE LAPPÉ, AMERICAN WRITER

The path of self-devotion leads us out of the realm of comfortable habit into a less familiar terrain where at times we might feel excited, at other times vulnerable or insecure. Our willingness to set foot upon this terrain stems from our deepest motivation. Think of the great explorers of a bygone age whose appetite for knowledge and experience had them hacking through jungles and rafting among white-water rapids. Now think of your own insecurities as you face the unknown. How many of them seem, fundamentally, to be rooted in the habit of comfort? Life in the comfort zone accumulates nothing but a hoard of waste. The path of self-devotion is the path of dissolving fears. Life lived to the full is always going to be an adventure, a journey of self-knowledge.

balance risk and reward

EXERCISE THIRTEEN

When you are uncertain about a decision you have to take, the following exercise will assist you in coming to a resolution. We do not always know what all the possible risks and rewards are, and we cannot foresee if the risks will be worth taking. Until you resolve this dilemma you will be stuck in an endless cycle of indecision, pulling your energy away from living and manifesting your desires. Ideally, get the answers to these questions out of your head and onto paper.

1. ***What is the worst thing that could happen*** *if you take the action you are unsure about? Is it likely to happen? If it did, would you be able to deal with it?*
2. ***What is the best thing that could happen?*** *Again, ask yourself if it is likely to happen, and if it did, how that would be for you.*
3. ***Is there anything you can do*** *to help things go the way you want? If so, take action.*
4. ***Imagine your life six months from now,*** *having taken the risk. Will this decision still matter in six months' time?*
5. ***Imagine sitting in your rocking chair*** *on your front porch in old age. Will the decision matter then? Will taking this risk or not taking this risk create any regrets for you?*

dissolve the inner barriers

Sometimes our biggest roadblocks take up space between our ears. Ingrained in our minds are factors that interfere with our ability to be all that we desire to be. Most of these internal barriers fall into one of two categories: self-sabotaging beliefs and, akin to these, self-sabotaging patterns of behaviour.

My secret is positive thinking and no drinking.

MAE WEST, AMERICAN ACTRESS

Self-sabotaging beliefs are those we hold on to even though they no longer serve us. They tell us how we are not capable enough, not clever enough, not creative enough. For example, there might have been a time when you were in a difficult relationship with a difficult person. Instead of trying to work through the situation, you decided, as was your right, that the relationship was not worth the hassle, and you left. Inadvertently, you may have walked away with the belief that you can't handle relationships, or that you have a tendency to quit when things get tough, or that you are unreliable. Even though you did the best you could in a bad situation, your unconscious mind skewed your perceptions and left you this self-sabotaging belief that you still struggle with today. Now, every time you begin a relationship, you are afraid that something will go wrong or that you will one day break it off—and this belief could even prevent you from entering into a relationship at all.

Then there are self-sabotaging patterns of behaviour—things we do consistently, habitually, that interfere with our living a full life and manifesting our desires. Addictions to alcohol, gambling and drugs are all

a program for change

EXERCISE FOURTEEN

To break the ingrained behaviour patterns that do not work for us—such as getting upset easily, sleeping in every day, or spending too much time on the internet—we first need to become aware of those behaviours, and then choose to change them. The following exercise is all about implementing a personal program for change.

1. ***Pick a behaviour you want to change.*** *Let's say, for example, that you do not want to spend so much time alone at home.*
2. ***Write out all the possible solutions*** *to that challenge. You could start a class, take a job at night, spend some evenings at the local coffee shop, invite friends over for dinner once a week. These are just some of the many ideas you might come up with. Write them all out until you have exhausted all your thoughts.*
3. ***Identify three steps toward change:*** *first the easiest, then the one that you are most interested in, then the one that will make the most difference for you. Schedule the steps in that order, and take them in turn. As you do so, the momentum of change is building. Track your success over the days and weeks. At the end of each week, plan for the next week.*

examples of severe self-sabotaging patterns. If you suspect that you have an addiction, don't be ashamed of it—we are all human and fallible, and addiction can happen to anyone. Ask someone you trust—a good friend or a close family member—to help you. That is all I can say here, as addiction is outside the scope of this book.

Less severe self-sabotaging patterns include constantly being in a rush in a way that leaves you anxious and frustrated; always turning on the TV for hours after work, instead of writing those letters or planning or furthering that project; always declining social invitations, even though you want to expand your circle of friends. Do any self-sabotaging patterns come to mind when you think of yourself in this way?

name that person

One of the self-sabotaging beliefs people have about themselves—because they have been told it countless times—is that it is difficult to remember people's names. Remembering names is, in fact, easy: all it takes is attention. Most of the time we do not remember names because we did not hear them in the first place. When introduced to people, we are usually focused on their appearance, or the pressure of their handshake—because of these distractions by these thoughts, we fail to grasp their name. Focus your full attention on hearing the name, then say it aloud to make sure you heard it right. Later in your conversation, use the name again—and repeat it to yourself whenever you glance in that person's direction. Remembering a person's name honours them—as well as being a powerful way to create rapport and be remembered yourself.

As you travel the path of self-devotion (see pp.70–72), look out for beliefs and behaviours working against your interests. To eliminate habitual behaviour, see yourself as a gardener, pruning excess growth to improve your rose bushes in the future. Or in some areas of life you might harbour unfair prejudices against yourself: you might feel, say, that you are lacking in social skills. There is no point in merely living with this self-assessment. Either you are wrong, in which case a burden will fall from your shoulders once you realize your mistake; or you are right, in which case you will gain from striving to engage more with others. A self-sabotaging belief may be dissolved in either of these two ways. Zap it now: you deserve to be free of it.

the power of a physical image

Prehistoric people drew pictures on the sides of caves to communicate their deepest preoccupations. As important as words and writing are to power thinking, words alone are not the only effective way to put ideas into your head and keep them there. Think of the pleasure you felt the last time you watched a beautiful sunset, or saw someone you love walk toward you. Images generate emotions. And you can use these emotions to bring your desires closer to realization.

You have, of course, heard of those who display a picture of a thin person, or of themselves when their weight was lower, on their refrigerator to remind them not to overeat. Some teenage boys put pictures of cars on their bathroom mirrors, and children tear pictures of toys out of magazines for the whole family to see—a way of invoking the conviction that the toy will one day come through the door.

Early in my professional career, I participated in a new-member sales drive with my local chamber of commerce. Whoever brought in the most new members won two tickets to Paris. To inspire me to action, I pasted a picture of the Eiffel Tower onto the cover of my notebook to remind me, every time I made a call, how much I wanted to see the City of Lights. I won that campaign and visited the Eiffel Tower. Since then I have recognized and used the power of images to help myself and the people I work with turn desires into reality more easily.

Sarah, a writer of historical novels, commissioned an artist to create a cover image for the book she was writing, so that she could see her

create an image of your desire

EXERCISE FIFTEEN

Unlike a mental image, a physical image is something you can see and touch that can give concrete form to a desired situation, and hence act as a powerful engine, propelling you toward manifesting your desires.

1. ***Choose one of your desires*** *that is not coming to you as easily as you would like, or one that has central importance to you at the moment.*
2. ***Choose a physical image*** *to represent the realization of that desire. Ideal options are a photograph, a picture from a magazine. Make a mock-up or use an object that represents your desire—for example, a compass for a sailboat, or a passport for an exotic vacation.*
3. ***Put this physical image*** *where you will see it often—next to your bed, by your front door, on your desk at work. It must be somewhere easily accessible to you—it is important that you can touch it.*
4. ***Every day, look at the image,*** *touch it, imagine that it is already in your life. You are manifesting your desire. Imagine the experience of success.*

desire complete before she had written it. She placed the future cover on another book and placed this mock-up in front of her in her office. As she worked through her book, she felt as if she were simply filling in the blank pages, because she could "see" her book as already a reality.

Frank, an attorney, wanted to start his own law firm instead of always working for someone else—so he had a brass plaque engraved, like the kind that would grace the door of an attorney's office. On it were the words "Law Offices of Frank Meglio". Inspired by this token of achievement, step by step he made it all come true.

With two children now at college, Peggy, a working mother, had a secret wish to go to college herself. I suggested she go to a stationery store, buy a gold-sealed certificate and a frame, and make herself a diploma. She did just that, and looking at the diploma made her realize the strength of her desire. She kept the diploma in a drawer and every day pulled it out to look at it. Then one day she went to her boss and asked if the company would pay for her to go to college. They did—and now she has a real diploma.

All these examples have in common the power of the image as a motivator. Think of a tracker using the lens of his glasses to focus the heat of the sun onto a little pile of brushwood to make a fire for cooking. You can use imagery in the same way to focus the energy of your ambition. It works, because the physical image helps both our conscious and our subconscious minds get used to the idea that what we want is already potentially ours, that we are already capable of it—and that now all we have to do is make it real.

If there is something you would passionately like to happen in your life, conjure up a mental image of the situation you desire. Can you see yourself, inwardly, working at this new career, or living with this ideal partner, or inviting your friends over to inspect the project it has taken you years to finish? Some people say that unless you can imagine something, it will never happen. Yet we all know how difficult it can be to form a persuasive image of future circumstances: the dream, in any case, never quite conforms with the facts as they unfold. Hence the importance of symbolism—the Eiffel Tower, the book cover, the brass plaque, the college diploma. Symbols effectively and unambiguously stand for the essence of things. They give you an image of the future, ready-made. They make the work of the imagination easier, leaving you energy to spare for the effort of making things happen.

On page 79 I've suggested creating a physical object that can help you create your desire. The object alone is not enough. You have to combine the physical image with your mental power to bring your vision into being. Take your object, hold it in your hands or place it in front of you. Sit comfortably in a quiet place. Breathe deeply and regularly, and relax. Now close your eyes and summon up an image depicting your ambition. Contemplate it for at least five minutes, allowing its power to enter your mind. Feel purposefulness flowing from the symbol into your being, like water nurturing a field so that its crop can grow.

where are you now?

In order to get where you want to go, you first have to be clear about where you are. At this point on your journey, take some time for a personal review. Indeed, make self-assessment a regular action, like checking your bank statement: at the end of the month it will help you to know what you can do now, and what you have to plan for.

The unexamined life is not worth living.

SOCRATES, ANCIENT GREEK PHILOSOPHER

Listen to what people say about you. Their feedback, even their casual comments, can give you new insights into yourself. Do you like what you hear? Are you flattered or shocked? Do you agree or disagree?

Listen between the lines. If someone says, "You should go into politics," they may not mean it literally. Maybe they think you are a natural leader, or very articulate, or a good mediator. Or that you are slick, less than frank, even a little devious! If you are unsure of someone's meaning, ask them to clarify. When someone tells you they like what you said or they like your work, don't just say "thank you"—ask them *what* they like about it. Once you are aware of what others see in you, you can build on your strengths even more.

What would you like people to say about you that they are *not* saying now? That you are reliable, that you get things done? It is worth answering the question, not because the opinions of others are motivating in themselves, but because they can act as a mirror, a way to check, indirectly, that you are satisfying your own standards. In the end, it is your own view of yourself that is crucial to your progress along the power thinking path.

the personal review quiz

EXERCISE SIXTEEN

Complete this quiz to give yourself an overview of where you are now.

1. ***Select a new page in your power thinking journal*** *to do the personal review quiz below. Write down any ideas that come to mind. Re-read the questions, then put the journal down, asking your subconscious mind to continue working on them.*
2. ***Return to the questions*** *in your journal over the next two days. Mull them over in the interim. You will find that on day 2 and day 3 you will have further new answers.*
3. ***On day 4,*** *after each response, write down what action you want to take.*
4. ***Now start to do it!*** *Set to work on bringing about the changes you seek.*
5. ***Personal review quiz***
   - **a.** *What am I tolerating?*
   - **b.** *What makes me happy?*
   - **c.** *What lie do I keep telling myself?*
   - **d.** *What is it time to let go of?*
   - **e.** *Where am I struggling?*
   - **f.** *What is missing from my life?*
   - **g.** *What am I hiding?*
   - **h.** *What needs to be healed?*
   - **i.** *What needs to be said?*
   - **j.** *What desires am I neglecting?*

thinking into action

CHAPTER FOUR

Would you sit on your couch sipping tea and eating a cookie while your house burned around you? Of course not. You would run out into the street as fast as you could and you would not stop to think about it. Your purpose and intention would be clear and you would not care what you looked like, what you left behind, or which door led you to safety.

With most situations in life we spend far too much time considering all the options and "getting ready to get ready", before taking action to make things happen. Reflection and planning are important, yet they are of no use unless followed by action. Thinking has a tendency to continue beyond its optimum threshold, like quick-drying cement hardening before you can use it. Don't let this happen. Select the action required, then take it without delay. Action is the power tool for transforming wishes into reality.

In this chapter we find out how to make empowering decisions so that we can turn our thoughts into reality; we discover how to learn from the power potential of others; and we explore how success breeds success—how our positive actions inspire us to become ever more fulfilled.

making thoughts real

Actions always need an emotional springboard. They cannot emerge out of nowhere, out of a clear blue mental sky. Behind any action there is always a will, which stems from an attitude, which stems from your belief in yourself. Get into the habit of making daily affirmative power statements, as described opposite. They put you into a state of readiness—to act when action is needed, to seize good opportunities as they occur.

> *The devotion of thought to an honest achievement makes the achievement possible.*
>
> MARY BAKER EDDY, AMERICAN THEOLOGIAN

Between thought and action, language can serve as a bridge. By recognizing this, we can see the key role that language plays for anyone who practises power thinking.

Are there thoughts you have haboured for a long time without articulating them, even to yourself? Perhaps you have secretly entertained the idea of starting your own natural foods business, taking acting lessons, or filling your nights torch-singing in piano bars. Maybe such ideas seem so improbable to you that you keep them in a mental limbo, not allowing them the validation of words.

You will only manifest in your life what you first manifest in your mind. However, your thoughts will remain locked inside you, far from the realm of reality, unless you animate them by sending them into the world as language. Thoughts fade or distort unless they are expressed. Speaking and writing down your thoughts endow them with life. The more you speak and write down your desires and ambitions, the more opportunities for realization you give them.

make your power statements

EXERCISE SEVENTEEN

Power statements are declarations to yourself about how you feel and what you want in life. They put you in a frame of mind for action. Do this exercise every day, seven days a week. Examples of power statements are: "Every day I feel confident" and "My world is full of opportunities." Use the present tense and keep your language simple and vigorous. Make many statements to support all aspects of your life and character.

Option one, suitable if you consider yourself a visual person:

Stand in front of a mirror every morning and evening, repeating one or two power statements with conviction for at least five minutes. Look at your lips speaking with self-belief, your eyes burning with intention. See the image of your powerful self being reflected in the mirror.

Option two, suitable if you consider yourself an auditory person:

With soothing music in the background, record yourself on tape, mini-disk or CD repeating your power statements. Listen to yourself twice a day, in the morning and at night. Drink in your own message, like a magic potion.

thoughts into words

We have looked briefly at the power of privately spoken language. Below are three further ways to use language effectively in pursuit of your most dearly-held ambitions.

1. Put it down on paper. To force your mind to retain all the details of your ambitions is a misuse of mind power. Instead, put your main ideas down on paper; and keep your mind free to create solutions and open up possibilities in response to what you have written. When you write something down, you can at any time review it, to remind your conscious and your subconscious mind of what you want them to be working on. And every time you come back to a point, you can continue to make refinements. According to the Austrian philosopher Ludwig Wittgenstein, there is nothing that can be thought that cannot be expressed. If our thoughts often seem muddled, this is because they are only half-formed. Language is the oxygen of thinking: it allows thoughts to breath and live, to become full-bodied.

Practice and thought forge many an art.

VIRGIL, ROMAN POET

Your power thinking journal is the ideal medium to support this process. Nevertheless, if a pen and paper are too antiquated for you, tap your thoughts on a computer keyboard. Although you might be tempted to record them onto an audiocassette, bear in mind that the eye is a better tool for scanning than the ear. Moreover, in a word-processing document or in your journal, you can embellish text graphically, with arrows and underlinings to highlight ideas. You can also use different colours to keep track of your revisions over time.

2. Make a "power" statement. Power statements (see p.87) are affirmations of an attitude, an all-purpose positivism that will serve any of your ambitions. My personal power statement is "Expect success!"—to remind me always to be ready to realize my dreams. Extend this idea to more specific situations. What would work for you? Take some of your key words relating to your ambition and use them in a phrase or slogan as a daily declaration of your chosen path. There is power in hearing yourself say aloud what you are working on creating for yourself. Say it like you mean it, say it like it matters, and memorize it—so that at quiet times in the day you can recite it in your head.

3. Use the power of witness. Have you ever told someone about something you secretly desired, then realized after you spoke the words that your desire has become even stronger? There is power in having someone else witness a declaration of your desires. Whenever you hear "Great idea!" or "Go for it!" feed on the enthusiasm. If anyone laughs at your plans, let their laughter make you more resolute. Share your ambitions as often as possible—and you will find them being realized.

a time to act

We must use time as a tool, not as a couch.

JOHN F. KENNEDY, FORMER AMERICAN PRESIDENT

Every day you have places to go, people to see, interruptions to deal with. You can do all the planning you want, and have the best of intentions, but it will all come to nothing if you do not also make the time to take the actions you have planned for yourself. Time is your best friend or your worst foe, depending on how you manage it. To improve your use of time and clear the way for you to accomplish what you desire—while enjoying the process—consider the following strategies:

1. Make a crunch time. Having worked with hundreds of people on time management, I know quite a few tips. The best advice I can give, the one that will make the most significant impact on your schedule, is to create your own "time crunch"—or artificial deadline.

You can allow an hour and a half to get ready for the opera, or you can allow thirty minutes—either way you will easily fill the time slot with all the things you need to do. Activities often expand or contract according to how much time you have allotted for their completion. Play a game with yourself. Give yourself artificial deadlines. This will also help you get to those chores you dread: knowing you have to do them only for a brief period, you will find them less offputting and you will feel such relief that you have got them done. Tell yourself you will clean the house until the pizza-delivery person arrives. Tell yourself you will fold the laundry until your date shows up to take you out on the town. By creating time crunches you operate with more focus. And you get into the habit of recognizing that time is precious.

When you have constraints on your time, your mind and body move in a more leisurely fashion, and you find yourself being lenient over interruptions, distractions and transgressions. Every day, incorporate at least two artificial time crunches—you will soon harvest the rewards.

2. Let go of perfection. Another challenge that prevents many people from being efficient with their time is a rule they are following of which they are often unaware: "It has to be perfect." When sending out an important document, yes, you had better review it before sealing the envelope. When you are giving someone directions, yes, it would be much better if they were accurate. Realistically, though, most things do not have to be done with the level of precision required for filling out a loan application form.

Whoever thinks a faultless thing to see, Thinks what ne'er was, nor is, nor e'er shall be.

ALEXANDER POPE, ENGLISH WRITER

Make the bed quickly—unless you're in the military, you don't need to be able to bounce a quarter on it. If you don't have enough of your favourite red plates for the table, you do not have to run out and buy more; be satisfied with using some of the orange plates instead. If you think an intention to have everything perfect plagues you, pay attention to this and be willing sometimes to let things simply be *satisfactory*. You will quickly find out how much time and energy this saves you.

3. Delegate. You have heard the adage that "time is money". If you earn fifty dollars an hour and you spend ten hours a week doing data entry, which is regularly priced at twenty dollars an hour, your employers are spending three hundred dollars more than they have to on data entry every week. Now apply this thinking to your home life. If you have only thirty waking hours per weekend at home, and you spend fifteen of those hours cleaning, running errands and cutting the grass, you have spent fifty percent of your leisure or family time doing chores.

I am going to let you in on a big secret: you are not the best person to do everything in your life. There are many things that need to get done that you don't always have to do yourself. Your time is best spent doing those things that *only* you can do. Only you can take yourself to

the sweet smell of success

If you are able to free up some more "you-time", spend some of it finding out about aromatherapy. It is a great tool that you can use anytime to create or boost a mood and help you focus on what you want to do at that point. Boil a pot of water, turn off the heat and add a few drops of a pure essential oil to the water. The rising steam will diffuse the fragrance around the room. An aromatherapy diffuser or burner will have the same effect. When you want to lift your mood, try lavender essential oil. Tangerine, lemon, grapefruit and other citrus oils are great when you want to be energized into action. For a more meditative atmosphere for insight or planning, use frankincense. For romance, go with rose or gardenia or ylang-ylang. Eucalyptus oil refreshes the air and clears the mind, as well as your sinuses. Find an aroma that is right for you, and always read the contraindications on the label before you start.

the gym. Only you can interview for a job or spend quality time with your children or sweetheart. Do those things that you really want to do, out of inclination or duty—those things that really contribute to your fulfilment and well-being—and leave some of the rest to someone else.

You would not normally think that you were the best choice for servicing your car, painting your house, auditing your accounts, or fixing the plumbing or electrics. When you can afford it, why not hire other professionals for the jobs not best suited to you? Delegate, or find other solutions. With internet shopping you can get your basic groceries delivered regularly. Hire a teenager from the neighbourhood to mow your lawn and run some errands, arrange for a cleaner to come in twice a month. Look for creative partnerships with friends—one week you drop off and pick up the dry cleaning for both of you, the next week your friend does the same. Always, in the spirit of the "time-is-money" equation, place a value on your time—this way you will gain profit-making time, leisure time, and quality time with your loved ones.

By creating artificial time crunches, letting go of being perfect and delegating tasks, you will find that you have more time to work on manifesting your desires. Put this extra time on your schedule—actually make a note in your diary or journal indicating "me-time". Then, give your appointment with yourself as much merit and as much priority as the doctor's appointment you move mountains to keep because it is hard to secure. You and your desires are important. Give them the time they deserve.

feed on mind and memory

All our yesterdays are gone forever, yet they can serve us today. On days of self-doubt or low energy, call on the happiness of times past and use this positive memory to fuel your current pursuits. You can choose to be happy in an instant. Any time you feel the need, take a few moments to project yourself into a past situation in which you felt alert, confident, optimistic. Reconnect with the feelings you had then—you were the same person, and the energy you enjoyed is still available to you. Take some deep breaths, then by an act of imaginative effort send that positive energy to every part of your body. Spend some time reflecting on the following themes, and draw strength from your findings on each of them. Or do the meditation opposite.

There is no cosmetic for beauty like happiness.

LADY MARGUERITE BLESSINGTON, IRISH WRITER

PEOPLE Who has contributed to your happiness? Imagine that person inhabiting your mind, spreading contentment from a halo of light.

PLACES Where have you been happy? Imagine yourself enjoying quality time there, seeing the sights, hearing the sounds, smelling the smells.

DECISIONS What choices have you made that enhanced your contentment? Imagine yourself drawing upon the same reserves of determination and judgment that served you so well before.

ACCOMPLISHMENTS What accomplishments contributed to your happiness? Look upon these as benchmarks of success to which you can readily rise again. Your previous accomplishments are glimpses of your current potential. Imagine yourself aiming even higher than these achievements—and succeeding.

build a haven of happiness

EXERCISE EIGHTEEN

Meditation is another key way to calm your mind and body and sharpen your intuition. It does these things by an inner journey, not into the past (as described opposite) but deep into the still core of the self.

1. ***Find a quiet place, away from interruptions.*** *Sit comfortably, in loose clothing—cross-legged (if it feels comfortable) on a pillow or cushion, or upright with your back supported in a firm chair.*
2. ***Close your eyes,*** *relax your body, rest your hands on your thighs. Breathe deeply in a slow rhythm. After a few moments, smile softly.*
3. ***With each in-breath,*** *imagine happiness as a coloured cloud filling every cell of your body; with each out-breath, imagine all stress, sadness or anxiety falling away. Feel the happiness flood like a sea inside you. Continue for as long as you like. If you are new to meditation, you could start with five minutes, and lengthen the time in subsequent sessions.*
4. ***After your session,*** *take occasional deep breaths during the day to reconnect with the relaxed contentment that filled your body as you meditated.*

power decision-making

By now you will have started to make some important decisions about your life. Some decisions stem naturally from moods or emotions, others require a preparatory phase of sifting through pieces of evidence and arguments for and against. Sometimes there's a risk of getting ourselves into a spin, with all kinds of ideas going round and round in our heads. The most challenging decisions are best made with the aid of a pencil and paper. Also, there are decision-making strategies and techniques that can lead you more surely through the labyrinth.

The Greek historian Herodotus, writing in 450BC, tells us that the Persians would discuss important issues and make key decisions late at night when they were drunk, reconsidering them when they were sober again after a night's sleep. Similarly, if they made a decision when they were sober, they would reconsider it later when drunk. This seems a strange way to carry on—perhaps the underlying idea was that a decision was probably sound if it seemed right not only when they were in high spirits but also when they were in a more subdued mood after a night's revelry. In their own way, the Persians realized the basic principle that it is best to consider your options from different perspectives.

Difficult decisions can be stressful and create a sense of insecurity. Even the most confident of us will occasionally fall prey to a brief bout of "decidophobia": the fear of making serious decisions. When we are not sure whether or not to do something, and we put off taking action, we are passively letting the passage of time make the decision for us.

this or that?

EXERCISE NINETEEN

When you have a lot of things to do in a certain timeframe and cannot decide what order to do them in, the "this or that" method is a great prioritizing tool.

1. ***Write down all the things you have to do*** *in your time frame—for example, today at work, this week at home, before your friends come to supper, or before you go away. Try to limit your list to no more than ten items.*
2. ***Look at the first item on your list*** *and ask if "this" (item 1) is more urgent than "that" (item 2). If so, it stays where it is. If not, it changes places with the second item.*
3. ***Go through the same procedure*** *with the second and third items, then the third and and fourth items, and so on to the end of your list. Write out your reordered list.*
4. ***Now go back to the first item*** *and work your way through the reordered list in the same way, comparing "this" to "that" and changing the order where necessary.*
5. ***Repeat the process*** *until you get to the point where no items change place on your list. You will now have a clear order of priority for the things you have to do.*

Indecision is a silent enemy that steals many opportunities from us. You cannot decide what to say to a friend who has lost a relative, so you say nothing—a missed opportunity to give empathy and support. You cannot decide if you can afford to go to a convention, and by the time you go find the flyer on it, the event has passed—a missed chance to meet with colleagues and learn about trends in your industry. You cannot decide if asking someone out on a date is worth the risk of rejection, so you do not ask—a missed opportunity for a significant relationship.

Be proactive about making decisions. Unresolved decisions take up too much time and energy. Decision-making is a tool for time management and for staying organized. When we spend too much time on decisions, it is because we are afraid of choosing wrongly—although in most cases a wrong decision is unlikely to have serious consequences.

Begin by making relatively unimportant decisions quickly, to give yourself time, space and energy for the big ones. These decisions don't

arrange for action

Feng shui is the Chinese art of home arrangement in which you encourage positive energy to flow around your home so that you attract the things you want—like success and good relationships—and keep away the things you don't want—like poor health and an empty wallet. A common feng shui practice is to put a mirror behind the place where you keep your checks before they are deposited; it is believed that this will double your income. Do not put a mirror where you keep your bills for the same reason. To bring a relationship into your life, display pairs of things—such as two candlesticks or two heart shaped pillows.

impact on your life greatly whatever you decide, so you don't have to waste time considering every possible scenario. How much space does a bathing suit take up in your packing? Hardly any. Throw it in your suitcasc and forgct about it.

When facing big decisions, work to the answer step by step. If you find yourself on the brink of deciding randomly, you've skipped something. Don't be daunted, don't panic. You have time to work this out. Don't decide until you can let go of anxiety, which clouds your thinking. Use your mind like a tool, not like an instrument of self-torture.

the power of gratitude

There are friends who impact on our lives in beautiful and significant ways and for whom we are truly grateful. I am blessed to have one such friend in Irv Spivak. Irv was friendly to me early in my career, when I was shy and insecure. He guided me personally and professionally: he cooked me dinners, proofed my articles, gave me wise advice and introduced me to other wonderful people.

A couple of years ago I wondered how I could express my gratitude to Irv for his guidance and support, which had been so valuable. This intention was amplified by the fact that Irv was a bit depressed at the time—he had several health challenges and no romance or stable work in his life to distract him.

Gratitude is not only the greatest of virtues, but the parent of all others.

CICERO, ROMAN ORATOR, WRITER, STATESMAN

Irv loves to sit in San Francisco's beautiful botanical gardens, which he uses as his own "think tank". As in most parks, there are benches donated in memory of deceased loved ones with little plaques giving the dedicatee's name and dates, usually with a few words of tribute. I had an idea. Why not express gratitude to someone with such a significant public gift while they are still around to appreciate it? I contacted 120 other people who were grateful for Irv's contribution to their own lives and we collected $5,000 to buy him a bench at the gardens. We dedicated it on his birthday with a big surprise party, the guests including several friends Irv had not seen for a long time.

Irv now has his own bench to sit on, with his name on it. The plaque reads: "In Honor of Irv Spivak, who lives, loves and laughs well." We

practise gratitude

EXERCISE TWENTY

Gratitude comes from an awareness of how lucky and special you are to have had this wonderful event or lovely person touch your life. Do this two-part exercise to increase your awareness of all you have to be grateful for.

Part A

1. ***Look at your life:*** *Who are you grateful for? List ten people you know and write next to their names why you are grateful to them. Is your gratitude for something specific they have done, or simply for who they are? Describe their contribution to your life.*
2. ***Contact these people*** *and tell them what you wrote. Call them, write them a letter, e-mail them, or better—offer to take them for a cup of tea or coffee.*
3. ***For four of these people,*** *do something that will make them truly grateful. Pick something that would be a big contribution to their life—and, if possible, make it a surprise.*

Part B

1. ***Begin the daily practice*** *of doing a good deed for someone each day.*
2. ***Every day, write down*** *in your power thinking journal* at least *five things you are grateful for every day. Never put down your pen until you have come up with five things!*

did this because we knew that Irv would make his bench serve as a symbol and reminder of how many people love him and how significant a person he is. Since that day, Irv has said "yes" to life at every turn. When a friend asked him—a Jewish man from New York, who is rarely heard singing a tune—to join a Gospel choir, instead of saying "Are you kidding?" Irv said "yes". Now, every Sunday, he reaffirms his gratitude in song. Letting gratitude into his life and staying grateful has made his already rich life even richer.

There is always room for more gratitude in your life—more room for you to express it and more room for you to receive it from others. A doctor friend told me that even our immune system receives a boost whenever someone acknowledges us and expresses gratitude to us. Stress and depression are associated with chemical changes in the brain that suppress our immunity. By showing someone you appreciate them, you can relieve their anxiety and help restore their immune system to normal functioning.

The more gratitude you show, the more kindness and generosity you will attract, and the more you will have to be grateful for. Start to think of gratitude as something you expect to feel every day. A birdwatcher who has just seen an uncommon species is at their most alert, and more likely than at any other time to see another elusive bird. Similarly, if you show gratitude once, you will soon find a reason to show it again.

Your gratitude is multiplied with a gift. A little something can turn a quick "thank you" into a lifelong reminder of a special day, a close relationship, a simple kindness. My first love gave me a small Persian rug to acknowledge our relationship, and fifteen years later my heart still warms when I see it in my home. Last year, after an evening out with friends, one of them, Tom, gave me a framed collage of pictures from that night. It was one of the most valuable gestures of friendship I have ever received, and it hangs in my hallway as a daily reminder of the special people who enrich my life.

From this moment on, resolve to be an advocate for gratitude. Savour it as it comes to you. Spread it everywhere. Make it last for those you give it to.

your gratitude archive

Whenever someone sends you a note of thanks for something you did or said, save it—put it in a place where it can easily be retrieved. Collect these notes in a box or an album, and take them out and read them when your spirits need a lift. If you ever have a day when you cannot remember anything good you ever did, or anyone who ever appreciated you, take out your gratitude box or album and spend a few moments reminding yourself of your worth.

hold a generous heart

There are bound to be people you have been generous with, people to whom you have given your time, your resources, your esteem, maybe even your money. There are people you have done things for, risked other relationships for. Some of these people will have been grateful, others will have not even acknowledged your offering.

A grudge is an ugly, heavy burden to carry. You will have seen the pain it causes: relatives or once-close friends who haven't talked in years because someone did or didn't do something, for some reason, half a lifetime ago. The cost of a grudge is a life like a puzzle—for ever incomplete, with one piece missing.

Do not live your life with a piece missing. Forgive others. Grudges cloud the heart and the mind. As Jesus said to a crowd bent on stoning an adulterous woman to death, "Let he who is without sin cast the first stone." There have been times when you, too, have been unconscious of another's generosity—times when you did not say "thank you", neglected to respond to a special invitation, or allowed a kind gesture to go unacknowledged. Usually these lapses have been unintentional: other priorities distracted you, or you simply forgot. It happens. If someone does this to you, do not automatically assume that malice is present.

Anyone who approaches others in a spirit of giving becomes habituated to a generous lifestyle. The energy we give out amply renews itself. This is the principle of karma. In following the path of power thinking we opt, implicitly, to live by our own self-renewing energy,

rather than have our energy drained by the experience of being repeatedly disappointed by others. Admire those who set an example, respect good qualities where you find them, emphasize with, and support, the disadvantaged, but do not absorb others' weaknesses into your self.

In practical terms this amounts to letting go of grudges—they will slow down your spirit. Find energy in the joy of being generous, of being in service, without any thought of personal reward. If all this seems far-fetched all you need to do is try it. I promise, you will soon wonder how you could have missed this obvious truth.

choose to approve

Power is the ability not to have to please.

ELISABETH JANEWAY, AMERICAN NOVELIST

When is it time to approve of yourself and your chosen path? Once you have travelled a certain distance along it and you know that you are moving in the right direction? No, this is not the right answer. There is no better time than today. Yesterday is a memory, and tomorrow is a mystery. How are you going to be with yourself today? Are you going to be angry because you did not do everything you said you would do yesterday? Are you going to be unhappy about your weight, your income, your love life, your home environment? Or are you going to approve of who you are and where you are at now? We can put too much energy into disapproving of ourselves—and of others. Divert that energy into approval. Approval is a choice, and by making that choice we are exercising great positive personal approval power.

Recognizing that your life is a journey is itself a kind of approval. Just as you settle down in a train or bus seat and do not become self-defeatingly impatient to get to the next stop, because you know roughly how far away it is and how long it will take you to get there, so too you accept where you are in your life, even though some of your goals might still appear very distant. Let us say that you are pursuing long-term changes to your career, or to your garden, or to your body. By not approving how things are today, by constantly wishing yourself further along in your progress, you add a lot of struggle to your life. If you approve of the whole journey, you can choose to approve of every stage of the journey. You can say "yes!" to today.

Whenever you make a choice, approve of that choice until you are in a position to countermand it. Suppose you opt to go to your friend's party because you offered to help her in the preparations—although on the night of the party you feel more like curling up on the couch. Choose to approve of your decision. Do not remind yourself all evening that you would rather be elsewhere. That does not serve you: it makes it hard for you to enjoy where you are. You're at the party—why not make the best of it by exercising your positive personal approval power?

And it is not only personal approval we need to be positive about. Getting worked up over things that you cannot control can undermine your ease and cloud your mind in an instant. Over time it drains your energy. If you are not crazy about a friend's new partner, don't dwell on it; instead, approve of their relationship and your friend's choice. If you don't like the traffic, or the weather, there is not much you can do about it—other than positively accept things as they are and find a way to make them work for you.

Filter your negative responses so that only the ones that indicate an appropriate action are allowed through. Where no action is possible, learn the power of acceptance. Approve of what you cannot change and find greater peace of mind.

the helping hand of chance

Adventure is worthwhile in itself.

AMELIA EARHART, AMERICAN AVIATOR

What you desire might be just around the corner, but if you get discouraged stop and walk in another direction, or turn back to the place you started, you will never know how close you were. Take this as the principle that keeps you going along your chosen path. And take any chance, however remote it might seem, that could lead to fulfilment. Follow up coincidences—coincidence is often the universe's preferred delivery system for making your desires real. Begin to notice and say yes to any coincidence that could move your life closer to where you want it to go. The truth is that you never know where the perfect connection that will plug you in to your deepest desire will come from. When a neighbour mentions that he heard you were looking for a bigger place to live, and has an idea passed on from his friend in real estate—listen, act.

Amy and John had been married for more than ten years and had always wanted to adopt a baby. They put the word out to everyone, signed up to an adoption network, worked with an attorney, and joined a support group for couples looking to adopt. The years passed and all the other couples in their group became parents. Amy tried to stay faithful to her dream, believing that her baby would arrive at the right time in the right way—yet as time went by, holding on to this belief became more and more difficult.

Amy's mother, trying to be helpful, told Amy that she knew of a woman who had adopted her baby after putting an ad in a small rural newspaper. She suggested Amy do the same. Amy was about to shoot down her mom's idea and tell her that she had already placed several ads in papers with a large circulation—with no success—when she stopped herself. Her mother was offering her a cue, a prompt, and by acting on this she might well be fulfilling her destiny. All she had to lose was a few minutes of time, a few dollars and—the biggest cost of all—a few further days of future disappointment. When our destiny seems to have stalled, this is usually the hardest price to pay. You must be willing to pay that price, over and over if necessary, to manifest your desire.

take a chance on action

In my workshops I encourage people to make a set of "action enhancer cards". They provide a fun way to spur you into action through a kind of "controlled" chance. Cut a sheet of plain card into 24 business-card sized pieces. On each piece write down one of your favourite verbs. Use verbs that are general and can be applied to many situations—such as, reach, express, enhance, proclaim—rather than specific verbs that apply to only one type of activity (such as, cook, dance or sing). After you have written on one side of each card, put your action enhancers into an envelope. On days when you feel you would benefit from a little boost, take a chance on your cards! Dip your hand into the envelope and, without looking, pull out a card. You have to do the action on the card as many times as you can during the course of the day. Think laterally: if you pull out "embrace" you can embrace a change, a person, an idea, and so on.

Amy quickly decided that realizing her deeply held desire of motherhood was worth that risk. She placed an ad in the newspaper that read: "Happily married couple wishes to adopt baby." Within days, Amy and John got a call from a pregnant woman. They helped her through her pregnancy until Zoë was born, and Amy and John brought their new baby home.

The universe will not wrap up your deepest desires in a gleaming gold box, tie it with a red ribbon accompanied by a notecard with your name on it, and place it on your doorstep. Your desires may require you to do unusual, innovative or even outlandish things before the universe is sure you are serious about your request. You might get many chances to realize your dream; however, most of these chances will go unrecognized because they will be delivered in a scruffy, torn paper bag rather than the velvet envelope we might envision as the perfect vehicle.

take a chance—take a journey!

A chance encounter may present an unexpected opportunity for self-growth. Do not ignore any calling to do something unintended, especially if it involves travel—sometimes you have to journey into the unknown to get back to yourself. Jill was excited about a trip to southeast Asia—she had been planning it for months. A few days before her departure, she attended a talk by a South American author. During the talk South America seemed to "call" her. She trusted the feeling, cancelled her plans for Asia and spent two years living and working in South America. Her urge to explore the unknown brought her a deeper understanding of herself—and greater personal power. Is it time for you to take a trip?

Was it a coincidence, fate, a miracle or simple happenstance that a pregnant woman who wanted to give her baby up for adoption read, and was moved by, Amy and John's ad? Who knows?—it doesn't matter why, where, or in what wrapping what you want arrives. All that matters is that you can recognize it when it comes—and you will, if you still believe in yourself and your destiny.

Show the universe that you mean what you say. Say yes to any opportunity that has the slightest possibility of providing you with your desire. You do not know how it will arrive or what direction it will come from. Be willing to explore all possibilities. Take a chance.

power from other people

My grandfather used to tell me, "Buona gente e buon macaroni sono uguali"—"Good people and good macaroni are the same." Why? They both have to be warm to be good. Think about the people who have influenced or inspired you. No doubt it was something positive about them that made them matter to you, and often this was their warmth—their friendly, open, welcoming character.

Worry less about what other people think about you, and more about what you think about them.

FAY WELDON, ENGLISH NOVELIST

The people with whom we associate influence our thoughts, moods and actions. If you are surrounded by warm, generous, proactive people who explore all possibilities in life, you are more likely to do the same. If you are surrounded by complaining couch potatoes, their slothful, excuse-filled monologues will wear you down by slow attrition.

I have a friend who is a police sergeant, and one day at his station he showed me a bulletin board covered with mugshots. Above the board was a sign in big black letters: "STAY AWAYS". These are people who have repeatedly been picked up by police for non-violent offences. Sometimes, as part of their parole, they agree to stay away from the neighbourhood where they have committed their crimes. The idea is that by avoiding their old associates, the people who influence them negatively, they are less likely to slip into their old ways.

Who would it serve you to stay away from? Who negatively impacts your attitude? Who criticizes you, is not warm to you, shoots down your ideas? Who makes you feel relaxed every time you leave their company, as if a weight has been removed from your heart? These are

relationship review

EXERCISE TWENTY-ONE

Complete this review to gain an insight into your relationships.

1. ***Take out your power thinking journal*** *or two sheets of paper.*
2. ***On one page,*** *write down all the people in your personal life: your friends, your family, anyone else you frequently interact with or give a lot of attention to. On another page (or the second piece of paper), do the same thing regarding your professional life.*
3. ***Look at each name individually*** *and, in turn, say each name out loud. Notice how it feels to say that name. Think for a moment about how you feel about that person and how you feel about yourself as you focus on them.*
4. ***Put a star next to those relationships*** *that you feel good about, that really contribute to you and enrich your life. Put a circle next to those relationships that you are not thrilled about, that drain you in some way.*
5. ***Review each relationship that has a circle alongside.*** *Ask yourself if there is anything you can say or do to improve this relationship. If you get some answers, take some action. If not, perhaps it is time to close the circle on this relationship and release it from your life. If the relationship is involuntary, and at the same time inescapably flawed, work out a strategy for dealing with it in the most effective way possible. Creating boundaries and limiting your exposure is a place to start.*

your personal "STAY AWAYS". Make a note of who they are—then stay away from them.

Now conjure another bulletin board in your mind, and above it a big sign that says: "BE WITHS". It is filled with pictures of people you want to spend more time with—people whose influence you seek. They have characters you admire, they have things to teach you, and they are warm. Seek these people out. Be with them more.

The best relationships are those that challenge us to be better people, teach us what living is all about, reveal to us the full potential of our own selves. However, in our high-speed world we are often so focused on cultivating our inner resources in order to work through our "to do" list that we overlook the most brilliant resource of all: people. Find warm, beautiful people and draw upon their power—associate more with your "BE WITHS".

Once you have identified who the most rewarding people are, how can you be sure that you are deriving full benefit from them? The answer is to make the effort, when you are with them, to draw out their qualities. Do something more together than merely catching up on news and views over a drink or a meal, or seeing a movie. Meet with the intention of bringing about a positive transaction of qualities, an exchange of personal strengths. One experience you do have, if all is going well, is *relish*: to find yourself positively savouring the blessings your companion is giving you, as well as, at the same time, taking pleasure in what you are giving. Below are some strategies for making things work for you in this way, to achieve the sense that in your relationship with yourself and with other people you are fully alive, fully powerful:

1. Share your wins. When you meet your friend, do not let "How are you?" or "What's new?" be merely casual formalities. Ask people sincere questions that will encourage them to share their wins with you. A win is an accomplishment, small or large—a promotion at work, a poem published in a magazine, a clean bill of health. Ask questions that aim directly for the summit, rather than circling endlessly around the foothills. For example: "What's the most exciting thing that's happened to you lately?" or "What challenge have you recently overcome?" I know this is a bit more direct and earnest than you are used to. It does not matter—I promise you, people love a question that allows them to really share themselves with you.

2. Be acknowledging. Tell people how you see them, what you appreciate about them. Tell them how you love their sense of humour, their intelligence, their insight, their kind heart, their great hugs, or whatever it is. To conceal such feelings cools off your relationship.

3. Make powerful requests. People can give you ideas and resources—only when they know what you need. Your warm, powerful relationships are a great resource. Use them as an oracle of wisdom, knowledge, experience, and as a mirror to know yourself better, to test your ambitions and convictions. Do not assume that they will not want to talk about the deepest things in your life—deepest usually means most important. The people close to you want to help you and contribute to you. Let them know how.

a pool of power

We have discussed how individual friendships can serve you in a multitude of ways. They can make you feel more fully alive, more engaged with the world. And they can provide you with a whole range of more specific and practical contributions, from a helping pair of hands and hard information to advice and emotional support.

All this will strike a familiar chord with those who understand intuitively the value of other people in terms of their own fulfilment. More surprising, perhaps, is the idea that synergy of this kind can be created consciously, rather than as an accidental by-product of friendship. There is much value in creating relationships that I call power partnerships—formed by mutual agreement to serve whatever purpose we want. A power partnership can help you practise a language, find a mate, or build a summerhouse. Whatever you desire, create a power partnership or two to get you there.

Even more potentially powerful is the idea of deliberately forming a group of people overtly committed to helping and sharing ideas, support and sources with a mission of mutual fulfilment.

Over the years, both as a facilitator and a participant, I have experimented with several group relationships created for purposes of collective growth, achievement, support or self-awareness. Some of these relationships have served to prevent me from making mistakes and others have been miraculously positive—showing me what can be possible when people gather together with an intention.

form a power group

EXERCISE TWENTY-TWO

Often we hold a higher sense of accountability to a group than we do to ourselves or to one other person. If you tell yourself you will schedule a mammogram, you may be more likely to be true to your intention when you know your power partners will ask about it next time you gather. The group energy adds momentum to our lives even between meetings. When forming or joining a group, follow these basic principles:

1. ***Choose your power partners wisely.*** *Will everyone bring value to the group? Will everyone show the same level of commitment? Is anyone likely to try to disrupt the group with a different agenda?*
2. ***Ensure that the group has a mission.*** *Without a clear and agreed purpose, people will begin to resent the commitment expected of them. Make a mutual declaration of intent, to which everyone is aligned—you can always change it along the way if necessary.*
3. ***Choose your number wisely.*** *There is more or less power in more or fewer people, depending on the purposes of the group. There will be group dynamics at work with any size. Experiment until you get the right number of people in your group.*

here sleeps the champion

Power dreaming—an unusual notion. When you talk about taking action, you probably think of things you do that involve physical exertion, however slight: making a phone call, going to a class, renovating your house, starting a business, and so on. Getting a good night's sleep is probably not on your to-do list. I encourage you to prioritize it, now. Your sleep time can also be your power thinking time. I am sure you have heard the old adage, "I have to sleep on it." Sleeping with a purpose is a valuable power-thinking tool.

If you think you're too small to have an impact, try going to bed with a mosquito.

ANITA RODDICK, FOUNDER OF THE BODY SHOP

The obvious reason is that a good night's sleep makes you more alert, awake, alive, enthusiastic. That alone is enough of a reason, as it allows you to be a better problem-solver, a more creative thinker, and much more fun to be around. To get a good night's sleep, observe the following watchpoints:

1. Do not eat a meal shortly before going to bed. There's a biological reason: much of the energy that would normally be used to rejuvenate your body is instead diverted to digestion. If you fast for a few hours before going to bed, not only will you sleep, you will also wake up more refreshed and you won't feel bloated in the morning.

2. Stop all exercise two hours before bedtime. Exercising activates body and mind, which is why it is great to do it in the morning—it gets

you going for the day. At night, it can keep you going when you want to stop.

3. Avoid caffeine and alcohol before bed. Caffeine, like exercise, is a stimulant and will keep most people up. Alcohol is a depressant: when you drink before bedtime, it can prevent you from dropping into a deep sleep.

4. Avoid stressful activities. Choosing the time just before you go to bed to discuss controversial issues with your family—or work out your finances when the coffers are worrisome—will cause your mind to continue to race after it hits the pillow.

5. Use your bedroom for sleeping, lovemaking and relaxing—not for writing reports, answering e-mails or planning how to remodel your kitchen. Engage in brain-focused activities in other rooms in the house. Associate your bedroom with sleep, not with productivity.

6. Use the hour before bed for winding down. Leave work and household chores for other times in the day; instead, read, meditate, write up your journal, or do something soothing. Soaking your feet in a tub of warm water is a great relaxant before bedtime.

7. Stick to the same sleeping schedule seven days a week. If you can find your natural sleep cycle and get into the habit of going to bed and waking up at about the same time every day, you will find both sleep and wakefulness are there for you when you need them.

Once a good night's sleep becomes a sure prospect, start to consider your sleep time as subconscious power thinking time—an interlude when your subconscious can focus on your challenges and ambitions. It will not really be you thinking about all these things—but your subconscious. Your own subconscious mind can be a strong power partner when you use it to help you advance your thinking and your life.

The last fifteen minutes before you drift into sleep are valuable creative time. During this period, remind yourself gently, and without making yourself anxious, of what you want to happen tomorrow or in the future, and instruct your subconscious to get the ball rolling so that this can happen. Ask it to begin to create a solution to the challenges you face. Brief it to plan your article, your proposal or your letter of resignation. Your subconscious will then put ideas together while you sleep. It is fine to do some visualizations, or to say some power statements or affirmations to yourself as you begin to drift off to sleep. What is not fine is to work on situations in detail—or, in other words, to do any external constructive thinking. Reiterate your self-belief, then set your subconscious on its tasks. Do not confront those tasks—your efforts will only rob you of sleep.

To derive full benefit from power sleeping, use those first fifteen minutes in the morning as well—after you've opened your eyes and the veil of grogginess is beginning to lift. This is the time to review your action plan and make your personal declarations for the day. The more powerful you can make your sleep and dream time, the more powerful your waking hours will be.

cue your sleeping partner

EXERCISE TWENTY-THREE

Follow this procedure for recruiting your subconscious as a power partner while you sleep. Do this any time, not only when you feel at a loss for answers.

1. ***If you are feeling thwarted in your life*** *and things seem uncertain, turn in early and see what a good night's sleep can achieve for you.*
2. ***Ask your subconscious an "inquiry question" before you drift off.*** *An inquiry question is one that does not demand a "yes" or "no" response, yet instead can reveal multiple answers. It allows the subconscious freedom to draw upon its profound wisdom. Examples include: "How could I have even more joy in my life?" or "What will allow me to be more fulfilled in my relationship?" In all probability your subconscious will work on the challenge while you sleep.*
3. ***In the morning, ask yourself the question again*** *and write out the ideas that come to you. Do not edit these ideas; simply write them down and review them later in the day when you are fully awake.*
4. ***Apply the same approach to specific dilemmas,*** *such as: "Shall I take that trip to Nepal?" or "Shall I specialize more within my chosen career?"*

wings for the angel within

Sleep can offer us an amazing degree of help in our lives, when our aim is to follow the path of power thinking. If you find this so surprising, it is probably because we are habituated to believe that the most fulfilled people are the most focused and the most effective. This is true, yet focus and effectiveness are not confined to the realm supervised by such faculties as intellect, reason and commonsense. These are important components of our toolkit, to be sure, but they are not the only components. Equally important are intuition, imagination, empathy, and other mysterious faculties that do not even have names.

Think of your full potential in terms of a person, a more developed version of yourself, inhabiting your mind and body and waiting for a signal to emerge, like an angel who emerges from a chrysalis. Imagine that person as having superior intellect, and being sharper and quicker than you. These are left-brain qualities. However, creativity and insight are linked with the right brain, and are no less important to realizing our full potential. What makes someone a brilliant artist, musician, comedian? We cannot say for sure—nevertheless, we believe in something they possess that goes deeper than intellect alone. We too possess this mysterious faculty. We know that there is more to us than meets the scientist's eye. Believe in the mysteries inside you. Trust in their power to work on your behalf.

take your thoughts for a walk

EXERCISE TWENTY-FOUR

When we walk, there is something soothing about the alternating rhythm of brain messages, muscle movements and sensations. Our sophisticated version of "Left, right, left, right, left, right" allows our deepest faculties to act as a corrective to reason and emotion alike. Use walking, as described below, as a power thinking partner—rather like power sleeping (see p.121).

1. ***Remove restrictions of time and space as much as you can.*** *Plan your walk for the morning and relieve your schedule of any commitments for that day. Decide to go wherever your feet want to take you.*
2. ***Select a topic****—some personal issue or challenge to reflect on as you walk.*
3. ***Put on your comfortable clothes and walking shoes,*** *and just slip out of your front door—or drive to a park or some other place of natural beauty.*
4. ***Walk aimlessly. Don't rush.*** *Enjoy the views, stop and watch whatever is going on, and listen to whatever power thoughts come to you. Keep going until you feel you are done, then turn around and walk slowly home.*
5. ***Repeat the walk once a week*** *or as needed to gain perspectives and find solutions.*

the open road

CHAPTER FIVE

Getting started on a journey to an unfamiliar destination always involves excitement, anticipation, and hope for a successful venture—or at least an interesting trip. Starting out, however, is the easy part. More challenging is staying the course, not allowing yourself to digress or be lured by all the distractions along the way. Yet, at times, *do* allow yourself to be a little wayward. Your life's journey is not a direct route: there will be many zigzags. Sometimes you will get to the next stage of the path sooner than you expected; at other times, you may feel that you have taken several steps backward. During such times it is OK to take a rest and stop for reflection. Then, once rejuvenated, return to following your path.

In this chapter we learn how to develop the resilience we need to make positive thinking a permanent part of our lives. We find out what happens, and what to do, when we hit setbacks; we remind ourselves of some of the most important principles that we have learned so far; and we conclude with some lessons in how to enjoy every step of this exciting journey.

the universal timetable

Unlike a track and field heat or a three-legged race, your life is not a competition. Your mission is not to finish first. If you intend to do everything in the shortest possible time, you will miss much of the texture of life—and in that texture lies beauty, joy and lessons to be learned. Often we create artificial deadlines in our heads that we try to match in our lives. You might have heard yourself say things like, "I'll be married by the time I'm 30," "I'll buy my first house at 35," "I'll be a millionaire at 40." Setting ourselves deadlines helps us with our planning and can serve as a prompt to action. However, conferring too much power on these artificial timetables and considering them anything more than a planning tool can cause inner turmoil. How much ease, versus how much struggle, do you feel in your life? Are you enjoying life and getting results, or do you feel a lot of pressure and believe that things are not happening fast enough? Struggle comes not only from working long hours, or trying to live a moderate lifestyle on a meager income, or functioning with sleep deprivation after childbirth. It also comes from wanting what we desire when we desire it.

The universal timetable is the cosmic circumstance, the thing that will always keep our desires and their fulfilment on different tracks of time. If you fight against the universal timetable, you will waste time and precious energy. You will also undermine your well-being.

Patient persistence can also be described, more mystically, as a trust that your desire will arrive at the perfect time in the perfect way. If you

are looking for the ideal partner, and you use a dating agency, giving up after ten uneventful dates could seem reasonable. Do not be reasonable: be outrageous, innovative and explore all possibilities. I have a friend who met the man of her dreams after 87 introductions: in her quest she received some astonishing rejections and propositions, and also had some fun. It was her faith in herself and her belief that her partner would arrive at the right time that kept her going.

There may be an aspect of your life that you have struggled with for years—you have tried everything. Now here you are: tired, maybe scarred, or at least a bit battered. Go find a cozy chair to sit back in and ask yourself if you still truly want what you have wanted for so long. If the answer is yes, then rise from your respite and start anew; if you realize it is not as important any more that is OK too. What is not OK is giving up and soothing yourself with disappointment.

It is good to have some sense of the category to which your particular ambition belongs. Some ambitions relate to finding the right combination of circumstances—the right job, the right partner, and so on. This is where patient persistence comes in, a belief that what you are looking for is out there, or that you can find a way to realize a specific vision, such as making an income from painting watercolours. You might have what it takes. Begin. Otherwise you will spend your life wondering.

changing gear and turning corners

We have been looking at such qualities as patience and persistence, but the time has come to state an incontrovertible truth: sticking with your initial plan is sometimes a mistake. Power thinkers are allowed to err, to miss the turn that leads to the true destination. After all, they have found in themselves the courage to experiment. And what is experiment other than a willingness to take the wrong turn sometimes?

You might be working toward becoming a yoga instructor, a fashion designer, a private investigator, or a high-school teacher. One thing these paths have in common is that their early stages involve gathering information (see p.68). We never know what an activity is really going to be like until we start to embark upon it. Moreover, we do not know for sure whether it will suit us as a vocation—even if we have some limited experience already, and even if we respond positively to a brief "job description", on the grounds that it sounds right for us.

Often, after exploring a particular path, the information we pick up will tell us that it is in our best interests to make some adjustments to the route, or even a complete turnaround.

In my work with people over the years I have seen how often what seemed like the right answer in the beginning soon demands a second look. So how should we respond when this becomes apparent?

As a power thinker, you will learn not to be discouraged when things do not go as expected. Instead, think of yourself as an inventor

Only the wisest and stupidest of men never change.

CONFUCIUS, ANCIENT CHINESE PHILOSOPHER

who relishes the quest for knowledge: finding out what does not work is as important as finding out what does. When something does not work, apply the following principles to gain a fresh perspective.

First, take a brief respite from your activity and get a clear picture of the current situation. Evaluate what is working, what is not working, and identify whether the change you need to make is significant or superficial, or whether it should be made at all. You might even decide to change the why—that is, to do the same thing, but for different reasons, repositioning it in your scale of priorities. Before shifting gears, gather all the facts. Talk to anyone else involved. Consider consulting experts. Do some free-wheeling, imaginative brainstorming. Write down all the ideas, and evaluate how each one might turn out. The creative process cannot be rushed: be willing to give your thoughts time to gestate. And be prepared to take an unexpected turn off your path.

resilience

In considering the skills of a power thinker, you might think about the need to be decisive, to be good at planning and time management, to be open and confident, to take risks. One vital personal skill that we often overlook is the ability to bounce back from setbacks—to be resilient. To be prepared to overcome disappointments is one thing. To actually experience disappointment, as an emotion, is something else entirely.

Groan and forget it.

JESSAMYN WEST, AMERICAN WRITER

Setbacks happen every day. The contract you have been working on falls through, a printing job is run with the wrong date, the person you are attracted to declines—graciously or otherwise—your offer of a date, the scales tell you to start dieting again. These might be minor issues, unconnected with your deepest ambitions. Yet on a day when your resilience is low, a minor setback can start to get out of control and even sometimes turn into a trauma.

Disappointment and dismay are both emotions, and potentially very powerful ones, but that doesn't mean that we have to sit there while the storm creates its inner wreckage. Just as we can train ourselves to combat jealousy, anger or fear (for example, through various breath control and meditation techniques), so too we can train ourselves to bounce back after a disappointment, mistake or misfortune. Take some time now to work on this ability to boost resilience. When a setback strikes, practise the following methods, separately or in combination:

1. Let go of what you cannot control and don't let the past hurt you. If you are stuck walking in the rain— enjoy the rain, even if it soaks you. If someone else obtains that promotion at work, you have nothing to gain by holding a grudge. In coaching businesspeople I have seen over and over that the salesperson who clings to disappointment, and turns it into a grievance, is the one whose sales will be down the next month and may no longer have a job the following month. Keeping your attention and energy on "the one that got away" is not a recipe for success. Power thinkers have no time for such self-defeating responses.

2. Build on previous bounce-backs. When major setbacks hit, such as the end of a relationship, the "keep going" formula won't work. Sometimes it can seem impossible even to get dressed and leave the house. To start living again, think about other challenges you have faced in the past—your best friend moved far away, you were made redundant and so on. Ask yourself how you dealt with these challenges. What worked for you then? Was it taking some leave, consulting a counsellor, watching *I Love Lucy* reruns, or joining a support group? Reflect on what has worked for you before—perhaps the time has come to try this approach again.

3. Make a choice. Years ago, after a romantic breakup, I spent days moping around my apartment with the curtains drawn. I was heartbroken. After a week of this I realized that I was feeling worse, not better, so I made a pact with myself: "No moping, only hoping." This didn't make things better immediately, but in time I began to see that the fog was slowly clearing. If you choose to get back on track, be patient—it will be hard at first; soon though, each day will get a little easier.

4. Watch your speed. A lot of people respond to setbacks by staying busy—throwing themselves into distractions and tearing along so fast that they have no time at all to think about the problems that brought them down. In the end, taking the escape exit and not addressing your emotions in this way wears you down, and in the process lowers your resilience to the minor setbacks we all encounter every day. It is better to face the facts and come to terms with them. Find the place in the middle between moping around and rushing around.

Success is going from failure to failure without losing enthusiasm.

WINSTON CHURCHILL, FORMER PRIME MINISTER OF THE UNITED KINGDOM

5. Let it out. When a major setback strikes, don't hold in your hurt. Do whatever it takes. Call a faraway friend, scribble thousands of words in your journal, punch a pillow or a boxing bag. Once you are in touch with your feelings, work on releasing them. Understanding and acknowledging your feelings is the farthest you can usefully take them. Once you have reached this point, the hurt will gradually start to diminish.

6. Rev up your rejuvenation. Self-nurturing, the time spent rejuvenating your energy, is more important after a setback than at any other time. Go get a Swedish massage, or melt in a tub of lavender suds. Do whatever deeply nourishes you. Make the care and feeding of yourself a top priority during times of personal challenge. It will ensure that you bounce back faster.

prepare your VIP visit

EXERCISE TWENTY-FIVE

It gives me great pleasure to play host in my home to friends or family who are important to me. I guess you feel the same way. Now imagine that the VIP is you. You are coming to dinner. Treat yourself like your most respected and welcomed guest. This is a good exercise to do as part of a resilient response to a disappointment or setback.

1. ***Pick a date in advance*** *and mark it on your calendar. Indicate whether you are planning a daytime or evening event.*
2. ***Ask yourself what you would like to happen.*** *Decide on the agenda. It might be a fancy three-course dinner, a bubble bath, a massage, a classic movie video with popcorn, or whatever.*
3. ***Put together your "to do" list*** *to prepare for your big event. Enjoy the preparation. Do not stress yourself by trying to do too much.*
4. ***Look around your house.*** *Is it ready to receive a dignitary? If not, get busy. If there is a lot to do, consider saving some tasks for the next VIP visit.*
5. ***Enjoy yourself.*** *All day or evening, treat yourself like the VIP that you are.*

the feel-good imperative

You are your own resource, your own partner, your own source of power. Whenever you are not feeling good about yourself, choose to make that a priority over any other issue. Get to a good place where there's a good feeling. Without that, nothing life has to offer will be as rich or as wonderful as it should be.

All of us have spells of low self-esteem, and even utter from time to time the agonized question, What am I doing with my life? After years of pursuing happiness, peace and self-understanding, I still have unresolved issues, of course, and some days I do not feel good about myself. The difference is, the days of not feeling good are far less frequent now.

A good laugh is sunshine in a house.

WILLIAM THACKERAY, ENGLISH AUTHOR

acknowledge yourself

Some of us wait for someone else to tell us what a good job we are doing, that we are a uniquely special person. Don't wait to hear this from others. Acknowledge yourself for all that is good about you, for your efforts and your successes. Take a pen and paper and make a list of everything that you have achieved today, large and small. Whether you passed your driving test on your sixth attempt, donated money to a worthy cause or simply filed away all your bills at long last, give yourself a well-earned pat on the back. You deserve it! If you still feel that you want outside acknowledgment, ask for it. If your boss, spouse or friend has failed to recognize something significant, let them know that you would appreciate their acknowledgment. (However, make sure you ask for it in a way that invites the person to give you praise, rather than makes them feel guilty for not already having done so.)

I know that these days are aberrations—like days of hail or blizzard. Such days can serve you, if you recognize them and let them be powerful catalysts for change.

Do not pretend that you are feeling good about yourself when you are not: that will only make you feel like a fraud. Acknowledge your feelings, and ask yourself what they are about. Once you have found the answer, you will recognize it as a signpost. Onward and upward!

This is the feel-good imperative—to be aware, when you are *not* feeling good, that you are receiving a briefing from your intuitive self, an order to break camp and move on. The way forward is not so difficult to find, because your own feelings provide you with a thoroughly up-to-date route map. Follow them, and you will begin to see what a brilliant navigator you are. You might not be as lost as you thought: a walk in the country, or a bowl of homemade chicken soup might be enough to restore a sense of equilibrium. Even if you have a long way to travel before you reach the path, your feelings will guide you truly.

manage your emotions

The trouble with most people is that they think with their hopes or fears rather than with their minds.

WILL DURANT, AMERICAN HISTORIAN

One year some friends of mine were visiting me in California from Italy. A friend, Stefano, was particularly keen to see the famous forest of giant sequoia trees. With much preparation we arranged a weekend excursion to see these magnificent trees, relax in a cabin and rejuvenate ourselves by the lakeshore. Stefano was exhilarated as we began our expedition. However, shortly after we set out along the highway, our car broke down. Without being unduly disconcerted, someone suggested that we make our way back home by public transport to pick up another car that was available to us. Everyone agreed except Stefano.

His face was flushed, his discomposure obvious to all. This trouble with the car, he said, was a sign that we should not persist with the adventure. He quoted an old Italian adage, "Lunedì e martedì, non si parte, non se inizia l'arte," which loosely translates as "On Mondays and Tuesdays do not begin a trip or a new project." No amount of reasoning would shift his position. Even though he dearly wanted to see the sequoias, he let his emotions rule him. The rest of us salvaged the expedition, while Stefano retreated to the city and remained there, thoroughly defeated by inner turmoil.

Emotions can pose a major challenge to all of us, and to attempt to control them is perhaps a futile undertaking. However, the management of emotions is something well within our grasp. Stefano's feelings were real and valid, yet he did not have to allow them to be more powerful than

his desire to see the sequoias. Whatever emotion you are experiencing—fear, sadness, frustration, rejection, shyness—that is OK. Your emotions are valid and real. However, they do not have to dictate your behaviour. Your will can be more powerful, and must be if you are to create the life you want. Emotional weather is something that happens: we cannot do anything to prevent it. But we can keep the weather outside, beyond the window. We do not have to let its rampages come into the house where they can hurt us.

To begin to manage your emotions more effectively, you must recognize the importance of what you desire—and that desire must be more compelling than the emotions you are experiencing right now. To achieve this conquest over your inner weather do the following:

1. Acknowledge your emotions. Left unacknowledged, your emotions will rant and rage like an ignored child. Once declared and given a bit of attention, emotions can soften and perhaps even dissipate. For example, take guilt. Fran, a college adviser, said in a workshop that when she takes time for herself she feels guilty. I suggested to her that she acknowledge the guilt and take time for herself anyway. Every time Fran acknowledges her guilty feelings and still takes time for herself, the guilt is diminished. Anger, too, needs to be acknowledged. You can then express it responsibly by writing it down or working it out at the gym. Telling someone what you think or feel is always an option, although this can damage relationships if you do not speak sensitively. Always consider the impact that expressing your anger might have.

2. Do not judge your emotions. Do not reprimand yourself for the emotions you have. If you experience desire as you look at your best friend's spouse in a tight-fitting outfit, don't hate yourself for having that emotion. If you experience hurt from someone's insensitive comment, don't judge yourself for letting that comment get to you. Any emotion you feel is a perfectly valid part of your experience.

3. Let your emotions pass through you. It is often said that hearing is involuntary, while sight is voluntary. We can shut our eyes but not our ears. Think of your emotions as more like hearing than sight. You have no control over the rush of feelings. The important thing is to let them pass through you without feeling that you will be carried away. Desire can lead to embarrassing or even dangerous situations; anger can lead to intemperate language or worse. Yet only people who are unsettled by

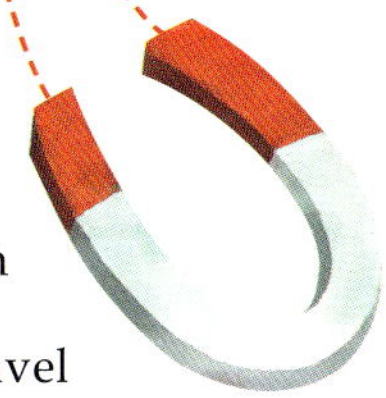

their emotions are at risk in these ways. If you acknowledge emotions for what they are—involuntary chemical reactions that in many cases have roots in past experience—you can allow them to travel through you like a rush of wind through a tunnel.

By all means think of emotions as inevitable but do not think of them as all-powerful. A power-positive attitude to life involves the understanding that cherished intentions are stronger than any emotion. While we cannot control what we feel, we can control what we do with our lips, our hands and our feet.

4. Eliminate fear through action. Fear is the primary emotion that prevents us from taking action, making changes and clearing up situations in our lives. Fear comes from not knowing if the action we want to take is the right action, the one that will work. Also, we are not sure if taking this action will result in some loss to us. We could lose some money, some aspect of our reputation, some self-confidence. These concerns, while they relate to perfectly plausible scenarios, are in an important sense fantasies—we will not know the truth until we take the action.

Have the emotion, and take action anyway. Every time we do not take action because of fear, we diminish our personal power, because the desire to take action continues to gnaw at us. Your success at this will grow with every step you take. It will seem like walking through a cloud into sunshine. Many experienced, successful actors say that they still suffer stagefright before every show. The fear is something they routinely go through. Once you learn what it feels like to burst through fear to success, you will wonder what held you back all this time.

the paradox of struggle

We all have struggles—difficulties we have to deal with somehow, for long periods. Struggles, in time, can even become part of our personality. Sometimes you hear people speak of others almost as if they *were* their struggles: "There goes Mary, the stutterer," or "I just saw Dave—you know, the one with the drinking problem," or "I ran into Kevin, the guy who never has any money." Such comments might strike us as unkind. Yet the truth is, almost unconsciously we too identify ourselves by such characteristics. Sometimes we have had a struggle so long, its familiarity and consistency comfort us like a warm flannel blanket. We would miss it if it were suddenly to be snatched away.

I have found the paradox that if I love until it hurts, then there is no hurt, but only more love.

MOTHER TERESA, HUMANITARIAN, ROMAN CATHOLIC NUN

It feels empowering to walk through a struggle and out the other side. We long for this freedom, however buried our longing has become beneath layers of habit. Often we can find release through action—and action can be scary. Take an example. If you have been in an abusive relationship, the last thing you will wish to do will be to start again with someone else. Your struggle is with the fear that your bad experience will repeat itself. How do you deal with this? Either by withdrawing into yourself or by working through the struggle. The latter course will bring you various kinds of tension in your life, but over time you will see the clouds beginning to clear. Bear in mind that nobody, not even a Zen monk, has a constant experience of sky-blue inner weather. Even on a cloudy day with a threat of rain, we can continue on our quest. There is much to learn and much to value as we do so.

go pearl-diving

EXERCISE TWENTY-SIX

This exercise involves understanding your struggle and finding the value within it—for every struggle has a value, like a pearl within an oyster. Dive to find the pearl: it will inspire you to live through the difficulties and come out the other side.

1. ***Ask yourself why the struggle is in your life****—what does it serve? What is its purpose? How does it help you to appreciate your life? Seeing what a struggle serves allows you to begin to identify its "pearl"—its value—and then release the struggle from your life. Write down the answers in your power thinking journal.*

2. ***Remind yourself of the value*** *that you found in previous struggles in your life. Perhaps struggling through school served to help you value education. Or did struggling with intimacy in a relationship serve to strengthen the bond between you and your partner? Now ask yourself what value you can see in your current struggle, and again record your observations in your power thinking journal.*

be an explorer

I think, at a child's birth, if a mother could ask a fairy godmother to endow it [the child] with thc most useful gift, that gift would be curiosity.

ELEANOR ROOSEVELT, HUMANITARIAN, FORMER FIRST LADY

Step out of the circle of what you know. This is an idea I encourage you to adopt as a heartfelt principle. Unless you devote some of your energies to pursuing possibilities for new input in your life, you will think the same thoughts and engage in the same activities, day in and day out. A power thinker continually searches for new ways to think and do and be. See your life as a great expedition. Be alert to the new things happening around you. *Make* them happen.

One day, while in Hawaii, I went whale watching. We were in the right place at the right time, and a huge whale swam right under the boat, came up to the surface and sprayed white, foamy water through its snout right in front of us. It was such an exhilarating experience. The next time I went whale watching it was wonderfully enjoyable—yet nothing could quite match the excitement of that first time. There is something really special about moments of personal pioneering, a sense of life unwrapping itself like a marvellous gift. Do you recall the first time you went whale watching, or salsa dancing, or painted your first landscape? No doubt a feeling of freshness, of participating in the unknown, permeated the experience. And if you were thinking as you read this, No, I have never done any of these things, then think again: perhaps it is time you did.

When you explore experiences far different from those that fill your everyday life, you gain a new perspective on yourself and the world. You might begin to see that some of your familiar anxieties are small in the overall scale of things. You might become aware of a new skill you never knew you had. You might find yourself inspired by the qualities of people or nature. Or you might simply have more fun than you have ever had before, and consequently launch a lifelong love affair with this new activity or interest. An introduction to Tantra, surfing, birdwatching or the ancient history of Mexico might be the missing piece for you.

New experiences can be immensely rewarding. Apart from their sheer enjoyment, they replenish your stock of memory and imagination, and can even make significant contributions to your future. Here are some suggestions for the would-be explorer:

1. Celebrate your curiosity. It was probably some Puritan long ago who introduced the idea that "Curiosity killed the cat." I'm sure they had it wrong: more likely, it is curiosity that gives a cat its proverbial nine lives. Curiosity can serve as your personal rebirth. If you are concerned about any dangers it might bring, consider this Tibetan saying: "It is better to live one year as a tiger than one hundred years as a sheep." Curiosity builds character. It creates powerful life experiences. It is to be celebrated.

Make a list in your power thinking journal of some of the things you are curious about—as many as you can think of. Do not edit the truth. If you are interested in cabaret singing, candlemaking or cross-dressing, that is great. Resolve to fulfil your curiosity about these things. Look at your list from time to time to remind yourself what you want to do.

2. Set yourself a curiosity quota. Each week, do something simply to satisfy your curiosity. Make it a fun game. Pick an area in which you have no experience, and plunge in to make your discoveries. Establish a curiosity quota, and fill it every week. If you find that you like being curious, raise your weekly quota to two or three items. You can even set yourself a daily curiosity target. Here are some ideas to help you fill your quota:

Read outside your circle. I know a woman who reads everything. She has no pets and yet she reads pet magazines; she has no children at home, yet reads parenting magazines; she is not African-American, yet reads *Ebony*. I myself have started to broaden my reading matter on airplanes. There is an aspect of harmless voyeurism in reading a magazine written for a group you don't "belong" to. It is fun, and you learn a lot.

One day, stuck on a plane without anything to read, I picked up a golf magazine. This was practically my first exposure to the sport. My imaginary stroll onto a golf course taught me quite a few things about the game that came up in a conversation the next day. You might not want to play golf, yet knowing more about it puts you in touch with something that is important to some of the people you will meet.

Take a new class. Often, the older we get, the more constricted our world becomes if we do not consciously continue to expand it. Going to classes on topics unfamiliar to you is a way to open yourself up to worlds of new possibility. Even if you do not stick with a new class, you are sure to learn something. Bear in mind that having a skill, even one that you do not have much chance to use, is an enlargement of yourself as a person.

Seek out different kinds of people. Do not make the mistake of assuming that the only people you can have a great conversation with are people very like yourself. Everybody has great stories to tell, and interesting opinions about life—although some are better than others at communicating. Take every opportunity to go where different kinds of people gather—a wine lovers' dinner, a meeting of local environmentalists, a bookstore workshop by a psychologist publicizing her latest book on dream interpretation.

Fight the "timid body" syndrome. Do you ever hear yourself say that you are too old or too out of shape to do something? That is an excuse. Nothing you ever do of a physical nature will feel natural the first time you do it. Be willing to look and feel incompetent—to be the clumsy one in a yoga class, or the last person to pick up a new dance step. Your new physical venture will one day seem as easy as driving your car. Do it, your body will adjust and you will be expanded.

powering ahead

Powering ahead is what perseverance in action looks like. Perseverance is what you draw upon when you are stalled or stalling as you pursue a goal or desired outcome.

The root of the word "discipline" is disciple. Disciples are devoted to what they believe in. Devoted people do what needs to be done to realize a desire, even when they do not feel like it, or when other goals impose themselves. Ask yourself: are you truly devoted to the vision you want to create in your life?

I have very strong feelings about how you lead your life. You always look ahead; you never look back.

ANN RICHARDS, FORMER GOVERNOR OF TEXAS

Many of the diversions you encounter will be worthwhile, and it would be unadventurous of you not to follow them. Then again, responsibilities, to family or friends, may set up an alternative parameter. If, as well as seeking to run a successful business, you have a sick child to look after, you seek to be successful at that too: indeed, it becomes a priority. The road often forks in this way, and sometimes the two routes do not join up again: the side turning becomes a highway in itself. However, a golden rule of power thinking is that you can power ahead on two roads at once—possibly even more. Obviously, when an unexpected duty or distraction comes to light, adjustments need to be made to your personal ambition.

Setbacks, struggles and slow-down will inevitably affect your power thinking journey. Sometimes an unexpected diversion occurs, or you may lose momentum for some less-easily explicable reason. Engage the following strategies whenever you feel a problem with motivation:

1. Re-evaluate what you are up to. Check that the direction in which you are headed is still where you want to go. If it is not, change tack. If it is, ask yourself why you want to pursue this vision. Make sure your answer is compelling, or another setback will occur again, and soon.

2. Get back to basics. Recommit, in your power thinking journal, to whatever changes you vowed to make before, and evaluate if anything has to be readjusted to help you meet that commitment.

3. Seek change for its own sake. When routine sets in, find ways to add change, spice and variety. Remain open to all life's worthwhile options and diversions—as you power ahead.

too much, too fast?

Sometimes, good things happen faster than we ever imagined. I coached Lynn, who received three executive promotions in nine months; Madeline, in her late 40s, who quickly got engaged and married for the first time; Jamie, who went from starving artist to sought-after muralist with one picture in a local paper; and Brad, 30, who went from garage geek to megarich with the sale of one software idea. If you find yourself suddenly swept away on a tide of success, and you are thinking: "It is all happening so fast that I am not sure I can handle it," slow down, take a deep breath, and work through it in your power thinking journal. Identify the adjustments you need to make—perhaps in many areas of your life—to accommodate the positive things that are happening to you. Check out any potential downside, seek to steady the pace, and meanwhile: power on.

find fulfilment

I don't want to get to the end of my life and find that I lived just the length of it. I want to have lived the width of it as well.

DIANE ACKERMAN, AMERICAN POET

Fulfilment is what most people, in their heart of hearts, are looking for, although it might not be the word everyone would use. We all know what this looking, or striving, feels like. Yet fulfilment is not something you find like a parking space, a misplaced sweater or an ideal vacation spot. It is something you *experience*, for fleeting moments, a day, a week, or months, even years at a stretch. While any one of us can appear to the casual observer to "have it all", that is often a glamorous illusion. True fulfilment is found within—although people, places and experiences can help you by reading your treasure map and showing you where to dig. To begin your search, here are some introductory signposts:

the fix-all solution fantasy

"Everything will be better when ..." If you have found yourself saying those words, then you may be a victim of the Fix-All Solution Fantasy. If you think your life will be perfect when you get a new job, a new partner, or a new, improved body, you are in fantasyland. Sometimes we live fixated on the thing that we see as most broken in our lives, and in the process we miss all the other aspects of our lives that need attention. While striving for one ambition, we avoid addressing the whole question of personal fulfilment. Marriage, a law degree or a new car will only fill the void for a brief while. Life is more than your most targetted ambition. Outer success is good and important—it builds self-esteem, provides security and often allows us to be creative. However, personal fulfilment does not come only from success on the outside, it comes from the inside and involves your heart, soul and head.

1. Make peace with your past. Accept the choices you made yesterday that have brought you to where you are today. As I have said before, yesterday is gone—you cannot fix it, you cannot change it, you can only acknowledge it. Choose to be the best you can be from now on. Have no regrets for yesterday only intentions for tomorrow.

2. Make peace with who you are today. I am saddened by so many fine people I see who are appreciated by others, yet cannot see their own brilliance. Embrace, love, honour, respect and nurture who you are today. Be your own biggest admirer. See all the value everyone else sees. Sure, you have room to grow—we all do. Let that not be a source of frustration. It is a source of value in yourself to see your own potential and take steps toward realizing that potential. In the meantime, hold the image of your best qualities in your mind, and be content with them: they are limitless fuel for your engine.

3. Make peace with where you are today. Fantasy is fun, yet don't spend too much energy thinking about what you would do if you had a magic wand—unless you use this visualization as a way to shape a positive ambition for yourself, with a view to taking firm and practical steps in that direction. Wishful thoughts without actions are wasteful thoughts. The reality is that your path has many turns, rest-stops, backroads and switchbacks. If you feel a surge of frustration whenever you encounter such features, the thing that is bothering you is life itself. What happens, happens—embrace it, enjoy it, learn from it. Contentment is more likely to be attained when you are at peace with the place you find yourself today, however distant your most clearly defined goals might appear.

travel beyond science

More and more people are taking a holistic view of life. Explore the wisdom of the East—for example, Chinese and Japanese views of the body's energy (*chi*) and the Indian principle of *chakras*. In Chinese medicine, pulse points on your wrist correspond to the organs and glands of your body, each of which, in turn, corresponds to different emotions. When my friend passed away and I developed a terrible cough, my acupuncturist told me that the lungs are associated with grief; and that strengthening them through acupuncture would address my symptoms and the emotional challenge they sprang from. If you are indecisive in your life, perhaps your gallbladder is weak. Or if you are feeling angry and aggressive, perhaps you need to energize your liver. Consider exploring acupuncture or another "energy medicine" to address any imbalance in your emotions that other solutions have failed to relieve.

4. Make peace with the universe. Many tragic things happen in this world every day. Some of these tragedies may have happened to you. You can blame God; you can blame the universe. However, does this make you feel better? No. Does it change anything? No. Blame is anger in a finger-pointing cloak. Take off blame, and try on acceptance. Only while wearing this coat can you move on. It does not matter whose fault something was. What matters is how you are going to continue from here. Are you going to pass your days blaming creation or its creator, or are you going to let go of the blame and continue your search for fulfilment? Blame is all about the past—and as long as you are living there, blame will continue to be a barrier to self-realization and fulfilment.

5. Find wonder and mystery. Philosophers grapple with questions about the meaning of life, whereas most of us just want to keep moving on our journey. But it is worth pausing now and then to remind ourselves of the wonder of life—not merely the fact that we wake up every morning to the inexplicable state of consciousness, but all the other wonders too. A sense of life's wonder and mystery reawakens our awareness of the privilege of being here that all of us share. In valuing that privilege, fulfilment inches closer. Perhaps we are already fulfilled without knowing it. Just think for one minute about each of the following: the inner design of our bodies; the stupendous drama of sunrise and sunset; the inexhaustible variety of plant and animal life on the planet; the mind-boggling distance of the nearest star. In such a world how can life possibly be dull? How can we possibly feel unfortunate? Life itself is fulfilment.

celebrate!

Celebrations add the finishing touches to a phase in life, a satisfying sense of completion. Not to mention a whole lot of fun.

Wealth is not his that has it, but his that enjoys it.

BENJAMIN FRANKLIN, AMERICAN STATESMAN, SCIENTIST, WRITER

Pass a summer vacation in Italy, and you will everywhere stumble upon spontaneous celebrations in the local piazza. To Italians, every morning, every meal, every cappuccino at the local café is a celebration bursting with passionate conversation and camaraderie. We can all learn from this, even if we are living in a neighbourhood that is far from Mediterranean in character.

In the modern world we work hard for weeks, months, years to achieve something. When leisure time comes around, the work involved in staging a celebration is often a big deterrent. There are invitations to address, the right outfit to find, caterers to contract, and so on. Often the people who make celebrations happen are so exhausted by all the planning, they do not even enjoy their own party.

Still, celebrations warm your soul. They are magical, memorable and nurturing. Focus on finding more reasons to celebrate and more ways to do so. As you turn your attention to this, it will begin to happen more easily and more often. Use these ideas to get started:

1. Celebrate the obvious. You do not have to wait for an anniversary, a birthday, the winter solstice, or Easter. Celebrate your new drapes with a gathering in your home; your friendships with an outing to a fancy hotel for afternoon tea; your life by lighting a candle in your bedroom or placing fresh flowers on your nightstand. Even a picnic in the park can become a celebration, when accompanied with BBQ'd chicken, exotic fruit juice, and potato-sack races.

2. Keep it simple. There is no shame in inviting friends over for dinner and sending out for pizza, or offering a buffet instead of a sit-down meal. What is important is gathering with people and sharing yourselves with each other. Add celebratory touches to everyday activities. Cards of appreciation given "just because", presenting a friend with an unexpected gift, or even taking time out of your workday to go window-shopping on your own are all ways to give a special feeling to an ordinary day.

What lies behind us and what lies before us are tiny matters compared to what lies within us.

RALPH WALDO EMERSON, AMERICAN PHILOSOPHER, ESSAYIST, POET

3. Create your own traditions. In my youth, every Christmas morning people from my neighbourhood would gather on a hilltop, sip eggnog and watch the sun rise. Every January I gather friends in my home to set our intentions for the year. These traditions serve as markers that allow time for us to review and be grateful for what has come before. Think of ways to accentuate the happenings in your life. Devise your own personal traditions.

4. Expand your celebration repertoire. If you have not been to Mardi Gras, Oktoberfest, a Passover dinner or a Gay Pride parade, it is time you did. There are as many different rituals and forms of celebration as there are people to attend them. The more celebrations you enjoy, the richer and more vibrant you will be.

bibliography

ANDREAS, S. AND FAULKNER, C., eds. *NLP: The New Technology of Achievement*, Nicholas Brealey Publishing (London) and William Morrow & Co. (New York), 1996

BIRD, P. *Teach Yourself Time Management*, Hodder Headline (London) and NTC/Contemporary Publishing (Chicago), 1998

BUZAN, T. *Use Your Memory*, BBC Books (London), 1986

GEORGE, M. *Learn to Relax*, Duncan Baird Publishers (London) and Chronicle Books (San Francisco), 1998

IDZIKOWSKI, C. *Learn to Sleep Well*, Duncan Baird Publishers (London) and Chronicle Books (San Francisco), 2000

JEFFERS, S. *Feel the Fear and Do It Anyway*, Rider (London), 1997 and Fawcett (New York), 1992

KLAUSER, H. A. *Write it Down, Make it Happen*, Simon & Schuster (London), 2001 and Simon & Schuster (New York), 2000

McWILLIAMS, J.-R. AND P. *You Can't Afford the Luxury of a Negative Thought: A Book for People With Any Life-threatening Illness – Including Life!*, Thorsons (London), 1991 and Prelude Press (Los Angeles), 1986

MARSHALL-WARREN, D. *Mind Detox: How to Cleanse Your Mind and Coach Yourself to Inner Power*, Thorsons (London and New York), 1999

OMAN-SHANNON, M. *The Way We Pray: Prayer Practices From Around the World*, Conari Press (Berkeley), 2001

PEIFFER, V. *More Positive Thinking*, Element Books (Shaftesbury, UK and Boston), 1999

ROBBINS, A. *Unlimited Power: The New Science of Personal Achievement*, Simon & Schuster (London), 1988 and Fireside (New York), 1997

SARK, *Eat Mangoes Naked: Finding Pleasure Everywhere and Dancing With the Pits*, Simon & Schuster (London) and Fireside (New York), 2001

STOOP, D. A. *Self-Talk: Key to Personal Growth*, Fleming H. Revell Company (Grand Rapids, Michigan), 1996

WHITWORTH, L., KIMSEY-HOUSE, H. AND SANDAHL, P. *Co-Active Coaching: New Skills for Coaching People Toward Success in Work and Life*, Davies-Black Publishing (Palo Alto, California), 1998

WIEDER, M. *Making Your Dreams Come True: Find Your Passion With America's Dream Coach*, Random House (New York), 1999

WILDE, S. *Affirmations*, Hay House (Carlsbad, California), 1989

WILSON, P. *Instant Calm: Over 100 Successful Techniques for Relaxing Mind and Body*, Penguin Books (Harmondsworth, UK and New York), 1995

index

acceptance 106–7, 149
accountability 117
achievement 64
  past, using to help power thinking 94
  visualizing 25, 64
action 36, 39, 42–6, 85–6
  categories of 42, 43
  perseverence in 146–7
  see also proactivity
action plans 40, 69, 70
acupuncture 150
addictions 30, 76
adventure 110, 142–5
affirmations (power statements/ declarations) 48, 86–7, 89, 120
alcohol 30, 74, 96, 119
ambitions 51, 66–9, 89
  achieving 64, 86
  categorizing 127
  formulating 51, 66–9
  images and *see* images
  information and 128
  reality and 62–3, 66, 67–8
  writing down 66, 88
  see also desires
ancestral imprinting *see* imprinting
anger 138
  blame and 151
anxiety 76, 96, 99
appearances *see* reality testing
appreciation 100–103, 104, 115, 149
approval 106–7
arguments 32
aromatherapy 92
assertiveness *see* proactivity
attitudes 36, 42–7
  developing positive 46–7, 100–107, 139
  influences on 16, 20, 22–4
  Personal Perspectives 16–19
awareness of feelings *see* feelings

background, and basic beliefs 16, 20, 22–4
Baez, Joan 36
basic beliefs 16–20
  roots in background and past experiences 16, 20, 22–4
  see also self-sabotage
"be withs" 114
behaviour, changing *see* change
beliefs
  basic *see* basic beliefs
  examining 57
  holistic 150
  see also attitudes
blame 151
blocks *see* inner barriers
burn-out 72
busyness 132

caffeine 30, 119
capabilities 14–15
careers 29
catastrophic thinking 46–7
celebration 152–3
centres of power 28, 31
challenge areas 28, 31, 65
chance 67, 108, 110, 111
change 26–7, 31, 75, 129
  decision-making and 26, 27
  programs for 75, 83
  speed of 147
choice 27, 51, 62, 107
  see also decisions
clutter 49
coaching *see* training
coincidence 108, 110
commitment 66, 70, 146
  see also self-devotion
communication 60–61, 114–15
complaining 42, 107
computers 88
consultation 129
control 42, 107, 138–9
conversation 60–61, 114–15, 145
cooperation 45, 116–17

counselling 58
creativity 122
criticism 52–4, 82
crunch time *see* deadlines
curiosity 143–5

daily power practice 26, 48–9, 87, 89
deadlines 90–91, 126
decisions and decision-making 51, 73, 96–9, 121
  change and 26, 27, 42
  past, using to help power thinking 94
  Personal Perspectives and 16–19
  Pragmatists and 18
  shared 45
  see also choice
declarations (power statements/ affirmations) 48, 86–7, 89, 120
delegating 92–3
depression 42, 102
desires
  allowing 20–21, 27
  fantasy and 150
  feelings and 136–7
  images of *see* images
  listing 27
  recognizing responses to 108–11
  understanding and deciding upon 51, 54–5, 56
  see also ambitions
destiny 108, 111, 126–7
development *see* personal development
devotion to self *see* self-devotion
diary-keeping *see* power thinking journal
diet 30, 118
direction *see* intention
disappointment 33, 130–32, 133
  see also frustration
discipline 70–71, 146
Dissenters 16, 19
documents, dealing with 91
dreaming/dreams 66, 81
  Idealists and 16
  see also ambitions *and* fantasy
drugs 30, 76
  see also alcohol

emotions *see* feelings
empathy 60, 61, 122
energy 81, 91, 94, 104–5
  attitudes and 105, 106, 107, 126, 150
  group 117
  sleep and 118
environment *see* space
evaluation *see* reviewing
exercise 30, 48
  sleep and 118–19
  see also walking
expectations, limiting 20, 36
  see also basic beliefs
exploration 110, 111, 142–5

fantasy 148, 150
  see also illusion *and* imagination
fear 36, 96, 98, 99, 139, 140
feedback 52–4, 82, 149
feelings 32–3, 130
  awareness of 18, 32–3, 134–5
  connecting with positive 94
  decisions and 19, 26, 96
  managing 18, 30, 33, 132, 134, 136–9
feng shui 98
finances 30, 31
fitness 28, 30, 51
focusing 27, 122
food 30, 118
forgiveness 33, 104–5
friends 94, 100–102, 104, 112–16
  celebrations and 152, 153
  see also relationships
frustration 33, 42, 76, 149, 150
  see also disappointment
fulfilment 148
future, visualizing *see* visualization

gambling 74
gender issues 23, 24
generosity 100–105
gifts 100, 103
glamour 62–3
goals *see* ambitions
gratitude 100–103, 104, 151
grief 150
group dynamics 117

groups, power 116–17
grudges 33, 104–5, 131

habits 13, 75
see also change *and* self-sabotage
Hall, Minna 44
happiness 94–5
see also pleasures
health 30, 102, 150
Hemenway, Harriet 44
Herodotus 96
holistic beliefs 150
honesty 135

Idealists 16–17, 18
ideals 23
see also desires
illusion 62–3
see also fantasy
images 34, 78–81
see also writing
imagination 81, 122
fear and 139
see also fantasy *and* visualization
immune system 102
imprinting 22, 24
see also upbringing
inaction 42, 43
as positive 48
indecision 98, 150
individuality 68
information 69, 128
overload 49
inner barriers 36, 37, 69, 74–7
inner voice/inner companion 13, 52–5
inquiry questions 121
insight 61, 122
inspirational objects 34, 35, 78–81, 103
instinct *see* intuition
intention 40–41, 56–8, 81, 85, 146–7
prioritizing 64–5
intuition 18, 34, 60–61, 110, 122

journal-keeping *see* power thinking journal
journeys 110, 125
as metaphor 58, 106, 108, 125, 142
judgment 20, 27, 32–3, 138

karma 104
key life areas 29–31, 65

language 86, 88
see also affirmations *and* writing
learning 144–5
see also information
letting go
of blocks 37
of clutter 49
of feelings 33
of grudges 33, 104–5, 131
of relationships 49, 113, 131–2
life areas, key 29–31, 65
lists, as step to change 27, 112–14, 144

Machu Picchu 40
meditation 48, 58, 81, 94, 95
memories, using positive 94
memory 76
mind power *see* power practice *and* thinking
mind-body-spirit practices 48, 58
mirror exercise 87
mistakes, admitting and learning from 128–9
money 30, 31
"more" lists 27
motivation *see* intention
music, use with power statements 87

names, remembering 76
negativity 19, 36, 107, 112–14

objects, inspirational 34, 35, 78–80, 103
opportunities, missing 98
overload 49, 72

papers, dealing with 49
parental influence *see* upbringing
partners, meeting new 42–4, 127
partnerships, power 116–17
passivity *see* inaction
past, building on 30, 94, 149
patience 126–9
people as resources 82, 94, 114–17
perfectionism 91
persistence/perseverence 126–9, 146

personal development 30
see also ambitions
Personal Perspectives 16–19
Peru 40, 41
physical environment *see* space
pictures *see* images
places 94, 100
see also think tanks
planning 42, 85, 120, 126
pleasures 48
see also happiness *and* self-love
POW (Personal Objective Word) 54
power, centres of 28, 31
power partnerships/groups 116–17
power practice 26, 48–9, 87, 89
power statements (affirmations/ declarations) 48, 86–7, 89, 120
power thinking journal 26, 39, 48, 66, 88, 147
awareness of feelings and 32
exercises using 27, 31, 57, 83, 113, 141, 144
power thinking spaces *see* think tanks
practice *see* daily power practice *and* power practice
Pragmatists 18, 19
precision 66–7
presents 100–102, 103
prioritizing 64–5, 97, 98–9, 134
private space 34
see also think tanks
proactivity 31, 42–5, 54, 98
see also action
psychotherapy 58
purpose *see* intention

qigong 48
Questioners 18
questions
inquiry 121
see also self-testing
quotations 34

reactiveness 42–4, 45
Realists 18
reality testing 20, 62–3, 66, 67–8
recording 88
recreation 29, 48
reflection *see* reviewing
relationships 29, 32–3, 74
attitudes towards 22–4
decision-making and 18
examining 112–14
finding new 42–4, 127
finishing and letting go of 36, 49, 74, 113, 131–2
reactiveness and 42
see also friends
relaxation 29, 48, 95, 119
releasing *see* letting go
resentment 32, 33, 104, 131
resilience 130–32, 133
resolution *see* intention
responses
filtering 107
speed of 45
responsibilities 146–7
reviewing 27, 69, 82–3, 85, 128–9, 147
risk 68, 73, 104
ritual 40, 41
see also celebrations
rules, making own 20–21, 24

sanctuary 48
see also think tanks
sectors of life 29–31, 65
self as resource 134
self-approval 106–7, 149
self-awareness 32–3, 56–63, 82–3
self-criticism 52–4
self-development *see* personal development
self-devotion 70–72, 77, 146
self-discipline 70–71
self-love/self-indulgence 27, 48, 56, 132–3, 134
see also desires, allowing
self-perception 14, 134–5, 149
self-sabotage 20, 36, 37, 74–7
self-testing and self-questioning 19, 23, 25, 43, 45, 57
for decision-making 73, 83
setbacks 130–32, 133
shamans 40
skills 14–15, 145
sleep 118–22

sleeping on questions/ambitions 69, 83, 118, 120–21
space 34, 99
use of 30, 34, 49, 98, 119
see also think tanks
spirituality 30
standards *see* perfectionism *and* rules
"stay aways" 112–14
Stoics 18
strategy 40
strength *see* energy
stress 102, 119, 126
struggle 106, 126, 140
identity and 140
valuing 141
stuckness 20, 21
subconscious, working on questions and ambitions 57, 69, 83, 118, 120–21
Superman/Superwoman 64, 72
surroundings *see* space
symbols 78–81
see also images
sympathy *see* empathy

t'ai chi 48, 58
targets 66
see also ambitions
therapy 58
think tanks (power thinking spaces) 26, 34–5, 48, 100
thinking
action and 42, 85
catastrophic 46–7
filtering responses 107
Personal Perspectives 16–19
pervasiveness 13
power of 13, 39
quality of life and 13
training *see* power practice
walking and 123
see also inner barriers; inner voice; *and* power practice
time 48, 76, 90–93, 126–7
ambitions and 39, 51, 68, 69
decision-making and 98–9
managing 39, 90–93, 98, 132
pondering and sleeping on questions/ambitions 57, 69, 83, 118, 120–21
power thinking journal and 26, 39
proactivity/reactiveness and 45
self-examination 56
sleep schedules 119–20
think tank 35
valuing 92, 93
training 28
control of emotions 107, 130–32
of inner companion 54–5
see also power practice
trying out *see* reality testing
twelve-step programs 58

ultimate questionnaire 57
unchangeability 107
understanding 51, 59, 62–3
upbringing 16, 20, 22–4

visions 25, 66
see also ambitions
visualization 25, 64, 81, 95, 150
see also images

walking 123
wanting/wishing *see* desires *and* fantasy
witness, power of 89
Wittgenstein, Ludwig 88
wonder 151
writing 26
commitment and 66–7, 86–7, 88
decision-making and 96, 97, 121
for release 37, 40
see also power thinking journal

yes, saying 102, 111
yoga 48

acknowledgments

Thank you to Judy Barratt of Duncan Baird, who made my dream of writing this book come true.

I express deep gratitude to my parents Tony Rando and Maria Gloria who have contributed to me in so many ways and have always supported my path with love.

As a student of life I have had many great teachers whose hearts and souls were, or are, as big as their minds. I am grateful for the courage they have shown me and for the many gifts of wisdom and example they have given me. I bow my head in respect and appreciation to Kaya Anderson, Larry Byram, Sister Pauline, Anita Stangl, The Mermaids, Laura Whitworth and Marcia Wieder.

Also, sincere appreciation to Maggie Oman-Shannon for her support of this project and to Peter Bently for his fine editing.

contact the author

To receive a monthly success article via email or to find out more about Caterina's coaching, training and keynote programs visit her website at **www.caterinar.com** or contact her by email at **cpr@caterinar.com**.